The Book of the
FORD ANGLIA AND PREFECT
(1953 onwards)
AND FORD POPULAR
(1959 onwards)

THE ANGLIA SALOON, IN PRODUCTION FROM 1959 TO 1968. THIS
IS THE ANGLIA SUPER VERSION

THE ANGLIA 105E ESTATE CAR, WHICH WAS AVAILABLE WITH
EITHER A 997 C.C. OR A 1,200 C.C. ENGINGE

The Pitman Motorists' Library

The Book of the
FORD ANGLIA
AND PREFECT
(1953 onwards)
AND FORD POPULAR
(1959 onwards)

Covering all 100E, 105E, 107E and 123E
saloons, estate cars and vans

Staton Abbey, M.I.M.I.

Pitman Publishing

First published under the title
The Ford New Anglia, New Prefect
and new Popular handbook 1959
Reprinted 1960
Second edition 1961
Third edition 1963
Fourth edition 1965
Reprinted 1967
Fifth edition under present title 1971

SIR ISAAC PITMAN AND SONS LTD.
Pitman House, Parker Street, Kingsway, London, WC2B 5PB
P.O. Box 6038, Portal Street, Nairobi, Kenya

SIR ISAAC PITMAN (AUST.) PTY. LTD.
Pitman House, Bouverie Street, Carlton, Victoria 3053, Australia

PITMAN PUBLISHING COMPANY S.A. LTD.
P.O. Box 11231, Johannesburg, S. Africa

PITMAN PUBLISHING CORPORATION
6 East 43rd Street, New York, N.Y. 10017, U.S.A.

SIR ISAAC PITMAN (CANADA) LTD.
Pitman House, 381–383 Church Street, Toronto, 3, Canada

THE COPP CLARK PUBLISHING COMPANY
517 Wellington Street, Toronto, 2B, Canada

ISBN: 0 273 36072 8

MADE IN GREAT BRITAIN AT THE PITMAN PRESS, BATH
G1—(G.4194)

Contents

THE 1959–62 POPULAR TWO-DOOR SALOON

THE SQUIRE ESTATE CAR. THE 1956 MODEL IS SHOWN

1 Routine maintenance

THE maintenance and servicing needed to keep your Anglia, Prefect, Popular or van in first-class trim and a credit to its owner is straightforward. Moreover, such time is well spent; it pays dividends in better running and in lower petrol and replacement costs, and it gives one a new understanding and affection for the car. Many readers, therefore, will prefer to undertake most of this work themselves. Your Ford dealer can tackle more ambitious work and major dismantling; he will be ready to advise you on any such jobs. As this work calls for specialized equipment and some degree of skill and experience (many Ford mechanics attend a course of instruction at the factory) it is outside the scope of this book, which is intended for the practical owner.

In this chapter the work has been summarized under the various periods, or mileages, at which the various attentions become due. More detailed information concerning each job will be found in the other chapters in this book devoted to the individual components.

The Cooling System. The water level in the radiator header tank should be checked regularly. On older cars it may be necessary to check the water level daily, whereas a weekly check will suffice on a car that is in good condition. The water in the radiator is under slight pressure when the engine is running and the water is hot; it is dangerous, therefore, to remove the cap under these circumstances. If it is necessary to do so the cap should first be wrapped in a thick cloth and turned progressively to allow the pressure to escape, before it is finally lifted off.

When a cooling-water temperature gauge is fitted the normal running temperature of 185°F (85°C) is reached when the needle reaches the "N" mark. If the gauge indicates "H," the cause of overheating must be investigated as soon as possible; the radiator may need topping-up, the cooling system may be choked with deposits of rust or lime or the trouble may be caused by mechanical faults, such as binding brakes or over-retarded ignition timing.

A common cause of overheating—or conversely, slow warming-up of the engine during cold weather—is failure of the thermostat (1 in Fig. 13 and 6 in Fig. 14) which is fitted in a housing to which the water-return hose between the engine and the radiator is connected. A bellows-type valve was used on earlier engines, but during 1963 this was changed to a wax-capsule type. It is easy to remove the thermostat after disconnecting the water hose and taking off the top of the housing.

When cold the thermostat valve should be closed. It should open fully when the thermostat is immersed in a pan of water which is nearly at boiling point. If there is any doubt concerning the condition of the thermostat, renew it. Experts usually advise automatic renewal of this important item every two years,

Twice a year, the cooling system should receive attention. In the first place, it is advisable in the autumn to remove the radiator pressure cap after a run (first making sure that the water is not near boiling point) and to drain off the water, flush out the system and fill up with an anti-freeze solution. If the water does not flow freely from the radiator drain tap the opening should be probed with a piece of wire to dislodge any accumulated sediment. A hose should then be inserted in the filler neck and water allowed to flow through the system for about fifteen minutes, until clean water issues from the tap.

Before flushing the system it is an advantage to run the car for a day or two with a proprietary non-corrosive flushing compound added to the cooling water. These compounds, which are obtainable from accessory dealers or from your Ford agent, will remove any deposits of rust or scale which might be sealing minor leaks. If anti-freezing compound is used without de-scaling the system, there is a risk that its very "searching" action may find such weak spots, with possibly serious consequences if a leak should continue undetected during the course of a lengthy run.

Protection against Frost. Only a proprietary ethylene-glycol anti-freezing compound should be used. Remember that if coolant is lost by leakage, topping-up the system with plain water will weaken the anti-freeze solution, thus reducing the protection afforded. It is advisable, therefore, always to keep, say, a one-gallon tin of water/anti-freeze mixture available in the garage for topping-up purposes.

While the anti-freeze can be left in the system during the summer months, it is advisable to drain it off in the spring since the anti-corrosion inhibitors which are incorporated in the ethylene-glycol mixture tend to lose their effectiveness over a prolonged period of use; there is also the risk that during the summer the radiator may be topped-up more frequently and plain water may be used if the anti-freeze solution is not readily available.

Tyre Pressures. The tyre pressures should be checked weekly. These should be maintained at the figures given in Chapter 8. If the pressures are unequal or incorrect, the steering, braking and road-holding will be adversely affected.

LUBRICATING THE CAR

Routine lubrication is a most important aspect of your car or van. Neglect of the simple routine jobs can cause expensive damage or noisy and inefficient operation. Admittedly the design of modern cars does not encourage the owner to carry out lubrication and other under-chassis work. The solution is to raise the front or rear of the car on a pair of drive-on ramps, but these must not be used when checking the oil levels in the gearbox or rear axle, since raising either end of the car will, of course, give incorrect levels.

The Engine. Every morning, or before starting on a long run, it is advisable to check the engine oil level with the dipstick. The level should, of course, be topped-up at intervals to bring the oil to the "FULL" mark. These checks should be made with the car standing on level ground and a short time should always be allowed for the oil to drain back into the crankcase; otherwise a misleading reading may be obtained.

The oil should not be allowed to fall below the danger mark on the dipstick or serious damage may be caused. If the engine is in good condition, topping-up should be needed only every 250 miles (400 km) or at even longer periods when the engine is new; a worn engine, however, will need more frequent checks. Remember, too, that the oil consumption will be increased in hot weather and will be quite substantially increased when long, fast runs are undertaken, as compared with the figure that one becomes accustomed to when shorter runs at modest speeds are the order of the day. Tests have shown that the oil does not attain its maximum temperature until the car has been running for approximately one hour.

Using the Grease Gun. The points at which it is necessary to inject grease are shown in Figs. 1 and 2. The hand-operated grease gun used by the owner is an efficient instrument capable of injecting grease at high pressure and overcoming considerable resistance in partially-choked grease passages. In order to ensure that the maximum pressure is developed, however, it is essential that the nipple should be thoroughly cleaned before the gun is applied. Another reason for carefully cleaning the nipple is, of course, to prevent any risk of grit being forced through the nipple into the bearing.

If the nipple is dented or otherwise damaged it is a simple matter to unscrew it and fit a replacement which can be obtained from your Ford dealer. In an emergency, however, it is possible to obtain a satisfactory seal even on a damaged nipple if a piece of light fabric is first placed between the nipple and the end of the grease gun.

EVERY 2,500 MILES (4,000 KM)

Steering Gearbox. All dirt should be carefully cleaned away from around the filler plug in the steering gearbox before the plug is removed.

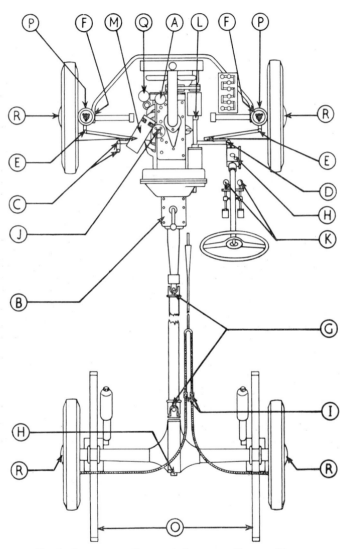

Fig. 1. Lubrication Chart for Side-valve Engined Models.
For key, *see* page 6

4

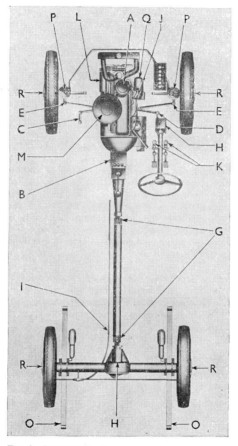

FIG. 2. LUBRICATION CHART FOR OVERHEAD-VALVE
MODELS. FOR KEY, *see* page 6

5

The level of the oil in the box should then be brought up to the filler hole, using only extreme-pressure gear oil of the type recommended.

Steering Linkage. The lubrication charts and Fig. 4 show the position of the grease nipples. Accessible from below are the track rod greasing points and the front nipple on the idler arm. The nipple on the rear bush of the idler arm may be reached from above. This nipple is often overlooked, resulting in the steering becoming very stiff and unresponsive. From 1966 onwards, nylon bushes are fitted to the steering connections and these do not require lubrication, but may squeak from time to time without indicating that anything serious is amiss.

Universal Joints. On earlier cars (before approximately April 1963) lubricators were fitted to the universal joints (*see* page 114).

Handbrake Cables. There is a nipple in each handbrake cable casing which needs charging with grease at this period.

Rear Axle. After the area of the rear axle casing surrounding the filler plug has been cleaned, the plug should be removed and the correct grade of hypoid gear oil added, if necessary, to bring the level of the oil up to the edge of the plug hole. A syringe fitted with a short length of rubber tube will be needed for this job.

Gearbox. Check the oil level in the gearbox and with a syringe inject oil through the level plug hole until it overflows. Some owners prefer to remove the gear lever by putting the lever into the neutral position, detaching the cover at the base of the gear lever and unscrewing the metal cap.

KEY TO FIGS. 1 AND 2

WEEKLY OR EVERY 250 MILES (400 KM)—*A.* Check engine oil level

EVERY 2,500 MILES (4,000 KM)

B. Gearbox—check oil level and top-up
C. Left-hand idler arm—2 grease nipples*
D. .Right-hand steering drop arm—1 grease nipple*
E. Track rods—2 grease nipples each*
F. Track control arm—1 grease nipple*
G. Universal joints (earlier models)—S.A.E. 250 E.P. oil or grease
H. Rear axle and steering gearbox—check oil level and top-up with E.P. oil
I. Handbrake cables—Lubricate
J. Distributor cam—a smear of petroleum jelly
Governor weights—2 drops of oil
K. Brake and clutch reservoirs—top-up with hydraulic fluid

* See *Steering Linkage*, above

EVERY 5,000 MILES (8,000 KM)

A. Drain engine oil and refill. Clean breather
B. Drain gearbox and refill
L. Generator—thin oil to rear bearing
M. Air cleaner—wash and re-wet with engine oil
O. Rear springs—spray or brush with penetrating oil
P. Front suspension units—check and top-up (not early models)
Q. Renew engine oil filter
R. Front and rear bearings—pack with fresh grease

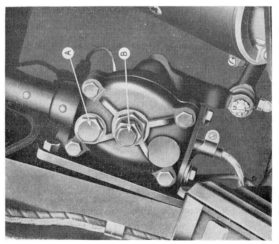

FIG. 4. FRONT SUSPENSION AND STEERING LUBRICATION
(A) Idler arm. (B) Track rod. (C) Track rod control arm

FIG. 3. STEERING GEARBOX, SHOWING (A) FILLER
PLUG AND (B) ROCKER SHAFT ADJUSTING SCREW

Oil can then be poured carefully into the opening through which the base of the lever passes until it overflows from the level plug hole. The gear lever should be replaced so that it seats in its socket and the two trunnions engage with the slots in the top of the selector housing. Replace the cork gasket and screw the cap down firmly.

Battery. The wise owner will have inspected the level of the electrolyte in the battery at regular intervals—say, weekly, depending on the atmospheric temperature, since the electrolyte will evaporate more quickly in hot weather. It is advisable, however, to check the battery also at 2,500-mile (4,000 km) intervals, adding distilled water to bring the level of the electrolyte to $\frac{1}{4}$-$\frac{3}{8}$ in. (6·3–9·5 mm) above the separators in the cells. The care of the battery is more fully described in Chapter 5.

Distributor. Remove the distributor cap by springing aside the two securing clips. In most cases the rotor, which is attached to the top of the cam spindle, can then be pulled off fairly easily by hand. If it is tight, it should be eased off by rocking it slightly from side to side as a firm upward pull is applied.

When the rotor has been removed a small screw which secures the cam will be revealed. A few drops of light oil should be placed on this screw, as a space is provided between the screw threads to allow the oil to lubricate the interior of the distributor. A few drops of oil should also be applied through the small hole in the distributor base plate, adjacent to the cam. This oil will lubricate the governor weight mechanism. Although engine oil may be used for this purpose a good upper-cylinder lubricant, such as Redex, is preferable. This type of oil tends to prevent gumming and also prevents the formation of rust.

A thin film of petroleum jelly should also be applied to the contact-breaker cam faces; this should be done sparingly owing to the risk of the lubricant finding its way on to the contact points. It is a good plan at this stage to separate the points by pulling the moving arm back with the tip of the finger. The points should have a grey, frosted appearance; they should not be unduly burnt or pitted, although the formation of a slight "pip" on one point and a corresponding crater on the other point is quite normal. Full information regarding servicing the points will be found in Chapter 4.

Brake and Clutch Fluid Reservoirs. These are in the engine compartment as shown in Fig. 6. Wipe the caps and sides perfectly clean before unscrewing the caps to check the fluid level. Top-up if necessary to within $\frac{1}{4}$ in. (6·3 mm) of the top of each reservoir, using only the correct brake fluid (M.E. 3833–C or Castrol Girling Brake and Clutch Fluid, Crimson).

Minor Attentions. Finally, after each 2,500 miles (4,000 km) a few drops of oil will benefit the throttle linkage joints, door hinges, bonnet hinges and other moving parts and joints around the body.

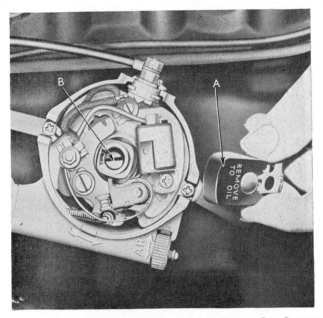

FIG. 5. REMOVING DISTRIBUTOR ROTOR (*A*) TO ALLOW CAM SPINDLE (*B*) TO BE LUBRICATED

EVERY 5,000 MILES (8,000 KM)

After each 5,000 miles (8,000 km) has been covered, certain jobs must be done in *addition* to those already detailed for the 2,500-miles (4,000-km) intervals.

Changing Engine Oil. The engine oil becomes contaminated with carbon and other products of combustion, including condensed water and fuel, and must, therefore, be drained out at least at 5,000-mile (8,000 km) intervals. If the engine is worn, the degree of gas leakage past the piston rings may make it advisable to change the oil more frequently; for example, it is usually recommended that a change at 2,500 miles (4,000 km) shows some economy in the long run, since, by maintaining the quality of the oil, the overall consumption is reduced.

The oil should be drained when the car has just come in from a run; being hot, the oil will be more fluid and will be holding in suspension the impurities just referred to.

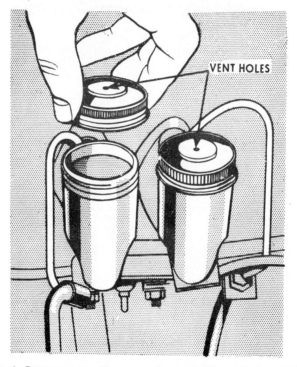

VENT HOLES

FIG. 6. RESERVOIRS FOR HYDRAULIC BRAKES (*left*) AND CLUTCH (*right*)

If a modern premium oil is used it should not be necessary to flush out the sump with flushing oil, as was often recommended with older types of car. As the sump may contain up to five pints of oil, a sufficiently large drain pan should be provided. An old kitchen washing-up bowl is a useful container for this purpose. Sufficient time should be allowed for the oil to drain completely before the drain plug is placed. The sump should then be refilled until the level is up to the "full" mark on the dipstick.

Change the Oil Filter Element. The centre bolt should be unscrewed and the filter element lowered as illustrated in Fig. 7. The filter body will contain a quantity of old oil which must be discarded along with the old filter element. Clean the filter body and fit a new element on the centre bolt with the flat end of the element downwards. A new sealing ring must be pressed carefully into the groove of the engine casting. The filter unit can then be refitted. Do not over-tighten the centre bolt because it will distort the rubber ring and prevent a good oil seal.

When changing the filter it may be an advantage on earlier models to remove the under-tray as it is not always easy to obtain a "first-time" fit between the filter casing and the casting when working from above.

The external type of oil filter is extremely efficient and it is obvious that it cannot do its job effectively when it becomes clogged. The usual sign of a choked filter is appreciable darkening of the oil. When modern premium oils are used, their mildly detergent qualities ensure that minute impurities such as particles of carbon are maintained in suspension. Such oils, therefore, darken rather more quickly than the earlier types of "straight" oils.

Oil Filler and Breather Cap. When the oil filler and breather cap incorporates an air filter, this should be washed in petrol and then dipped in clean oil. Shake out the surplus oil before refitting the cap.

It is important to keep this filter clean, to ensure good "breathing" of the engine, but sludge can still form on the internal surfaces and in the oilways if a second wire-mesh filter, in the bend of the breather pipe that carries fumes away from the base of the cylinder block, should become choked. This also causes heavy oil consumption, the build-up of crankcase pressure in the engine being sufficient to force oil past the crankshaft oil seals.

On overhead-valve engines the breather pipe is a tight push-fit in the crankcase, but it can be dislodged by placing the end of a piece of wood beneath the crook of the pipe and tapping it upwards with a hammer. Flush-out the pipe and filter thoroughly with petrol or parraffin. Subsequent attention should be needed only at about 10,000-mile (16,000-km) intervals.

Even when the points just mentioned have been attended to, sludging can be a problem if a car is used frequently for short runs in cold weather. In 1964 the amount of oil in the sump was increased by fitting a shorter dipstick, which called for the addition of about an extra half-pint of oil (raising the sump capacity to $5\frac{1}{2}$ pints or 3 litres). The later pattern of dipstick can be obtained from a Ford dealer or a $\frac{3}{8}$ in. (9·5 mm) spacer can be fitted beneath the existing dipstick flange.

A further modification on 1,200 c.c. engines was the provision of a larger external oil filter. Together with the dipstick modification, this increased the oil capacity of the engine by 1 pint (0·6 litre).

Carburettor Air Cleaner. When an air cleaner is fitted, it will require cleaning at least at 5,000-mile (8,000-km) intervals. The precise mileage at which attention is required will depend, of course, on the conditions under which the car is driven. Obviously, in dusty conditions the cleaner will require more frequent attention. The method of cleaning the filter is described in Chapter 3.

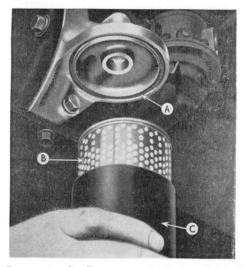

FIG. 7. DETACHABLE OIL FILTER WITH RENEWABLE FILTER ELEMENT
Later types of filter are basically similar
(*A*) Sealing ring. (*B*) Element. (*C*) Filter body

The Fuel Pump. The gauze filter screen inside the fuel pump should be inspected at this stage and cleaned if necessary. On the later Prefects a tap is fitted at the union between the fuel pump and the tank feed pipe to prevent leakage of fuel when the filter cover is removed or when the inlet or outlet unions are uncoupled. When no tap is provided, it will be necessary to disconnect the inlet pipe from the pump and insert a small tapered wooden plug. Alternatively, the small rubber cap normally fitted to the bleed valve on the clutch cylinder of later models (*see* Fig. 49) can be "borrowed" temporarily and pushed on to the end of the pipe. The bolt should be removed from the top of the fuel pump, allowing the cover to be lifted off. The filter screen may then be lifted out and swilled in petrol. Sediment should be removed from the base of the filter chamber by using clean rag that is free from fluff. When the screen is replaced the reinforcement should be uppermost.

The gasket that forms an airtight joint with the filter cover must be in perfect condition. Air leakage at this point will cause difficult starting and fuel starvation. If there is any doubt regarding the condition of the gasket

FIG. 8. FUEL PUMP FITTED TO OVERHEAD-VALVE ENGINES

A. Fuel tap (not fitted on some models)   C. Filter
B. Filter cover   D. Cover retaining stirrup

a replacement should be fitted. The gasket faces should not be painted with gasket cement or any form of jointing compound. The screw should be tightened home just sufficiently to make a sound joint; it should be firm, but not over-tightened owing to the risk of distorting the metal cover.

A point to watch with these engines is that the pump retaining bolts sometimes tend to loosen off, causing an oil leakage past the pump flange. The tightness of the bolts should, therefore, be checked whenever the filter is attended to.

Clutch Adjustment. The free movement of the clutch pedal will be decreased when the friction linings become worn; on the other hand, it will be increased if the clutch thrust bearing is worn. Wear of the friction linings is caused by excessive slipping of the clutch when starting the car from rest and when engaging higher gears. This trouble can also be caused by a driver slipping the clutch in order to avoid the necessity for changing

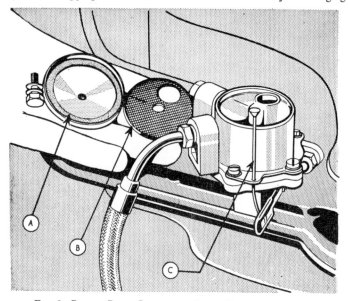

FIG. 9. PETROL PUMP COVER AND GAUZE FILTER REMOVED FOR CLEANING (SIDE-VALVE ENGINE TYPE)

The cork washer (*A*) must be in good condition and the filter screen (*B*) undamaged.
(*C*) is the hand-priming lever fitted to some models

down to a lower gear. Wear of the clutch thrust ring, however, is usually the result of driving with the left foot resting on the clutch pedal.

The correct clearance between the clutch release arm and the operating push rod can be adjusted as described in Chapter 6. If the clutch will not free completely, it may be necessary to bleed the hydraulic system as also described in Chapter 6.

Lubricating Front Wheel Bearings. The car should be jacked up until the appropriate front wheel is clear of the ground. The hub cap can then be removed with the appropriate lever and the grease cap prised off, exposing the hub retaining nut. Remove the split pin, retaining nut, washer and outer bearing. The hub assembly and inner bearing can then be drawn off. A gentle rocking movement should be applied to the hub in order to free it.

The old grease should be wiped away with a piece of clean rag that is free from fluff. The hub and bearings should be washed in clean paraffin, taking care to lay the parts out on a clean rag or on a sheet of paper on

FIG. 10. FRONT WHEEL BEARING PARTLY DISMANTLED
(A) Retaining nut. (B) Washer. (C) Taper-roller bearing

the bench in order to avoid the slightest risk of picking up any grit, which is fatal to any form of ball or roller bearing. The hub should be packed three-quarters full (leaving an air space for expansion), with a good quality wheel bearing grease and replaced on the front axle, followed by reassembly of the parts in the reverse order to dismantling.

The nut should be tightened up until a drag can be felt when the wheel is rotated. The nut should then be slackened back until the wheel is just free to rotate, with just perceptible end-float. This may best be checked by attempting to rock the outside of the wheel by hand. It should just be possible to detect the very slightest trace of play.

On later models, a more precise adjustment is possible, owing to the fact that the wheel nut is secured by a pressed steel retainer, which is in turn locked by the split pin, the combination being such that twelve different positions of the nut can be obtained in relation to the split pin simply by removing the locking ring and replacing it in a different position on the nut.

It should be emphasized that this adjustment is a critical one and that the wheel should be rotated during the whole of the adjusting process. Too tight an adjustment will cause rapid wear of the bearings; too loose an adjustment will also cause bearing wear and may adversely affect the steering. If in doubt it is better to leave the work to a Ford dealer.

When the correct adjustment has been obtained a new split pin should be fitted and the ends correctly bent back. The grease cap should be packed with fresh grease before it is replaced. After refitting the wheel, check the tightness of the wheel nuts when the wheel has been lowered to the ground. Then refit the hub cap and repeat the operation on the other front wheel. The rear wheel bearings must also be packed with grease, see page 18.

Front Suspension Units. The units fitted to earlier models were sealed and no provision made for topping up. On later models, however, a filler plug is incorporated in the front or rear of each unit, just below the spring seat. The level should be checked with the car standing unladen, on level ground. The correct fluid should be added if necessary to bring the level up to the filler plug hole and the plug replaced securely.

The bearing races at the upper end of each suspension strut are rather susceptible to rusting. It is advisable to remove the plastic cap on later models, or the pressed-steel cover on earlier cars, at 5,000-mile (8,000-km) intervals and to inject a small amount of engine oil.

Rear Shock Absorbers. The tubular shock absorbers fitted to early models and to the Popular require no attention, being hermetically sealed. The piston-type shock absorbers which control the rear suspension on later cars, however, may require topping-up at 5,000-mile (8,000-km) intervals. The level should be checked by unscrewing the filler plug and the correct fluid should be added, if neccessary, to bring the level up to the filler plug orifice. The design of the upper part of the shock absorber allows for expansion of the fluid when it warms up during use.

It is essential to clean all dirt and grit off the tops of the units before removing the filler plugs, as the slightest particle of foreign matter can put the shock absorber valves out of action. Since it will probably be necessary to use a torch and a mirror to check the level, it might be as well to leave this job to a Ford dealer.

Draining and Refilling Gearbox. The oil in the gearbox should be drained out from the bottom drain plug when the car has come in from a moderately long run. Refill with the correct grade of oil.

Draining and Refilling Rear Axle. Earlier instruction books tell you to drain the rear axle at 5,000-mile (8,000-km) intervals and to refill it with fresh oil. On later cars, however, no drain plug is provided in the axle casing,

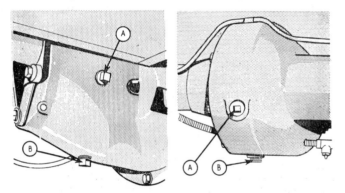

FIG. 11. LEVEL PLUGS (A) AND DRAIN PLUGS (*B*) ON GEARBOX
AND EARLIER REAR AXLE

as service experience has shown that periodical draining is not needed. This now applies also to earlier cars. It will, of course, be necessary to check the oil level in the axle at 2,500-mile (4,000-km) intervals as previously described.

Spring U-bolt Nuts. The nuts on the U-bolts that secure the springs should be tightened if necessary. At the same time check that any other accessible nuts and bolts beneath the car are fully tightened.

The rear springs are fitted with synthetic rubber inserts between the leaves. These inserts are oil- and grease-resistant and the springs should be sprayed or brushed with penetrating oil.

Generator. The front bearing on the generator is packed with lubricant on assembly and should require no attention in the ordinary way. Only the rear bearing requires lubrication and this should be done by applying a few drops of oil through the hole in the centre of the end-plate boss. If this bearing is over-lubricated the excess of oil may get on to the commutator, causing a reduction in the charging rate, or complete loss of charge.

Rear Hub Lubrication. Lubrication of the rear hub bearings at 5,000-mile (8,000-km) intervals calls for the use of a hub extractor to remove the hubs. It would be as well, therefore, to have a word with your Ford dealer before tackling this job.

OCCASIONAL ATTENTIONS

Under this heading it is convenient to group those jobs to which it is difficult to assign any hard-and-fast mileage periods. The intervals at

FIG. 12. CORRECT ADJUSTMENT OF FAN BELT TENSION

The pivot bolts (*A*) and the locking bolt (*B*) must be slackened to allow the generator to be swung outwards to increase belt tension. On later engines the free movement of the belt is measured on the upper run.

which such attentions are required will vary according to the driving conditions and the age or mechanical condition of the car.

These occasional checks and inspections are particularly valuable in enabling the owner to detect and forestall trouble. Small faults, which initially may only reduce efficiency, can lead in the end to more serious and expensive breakdowns. By keeping the engine clean, for example, oil leaks can be detected, while the removal of the accumulated road dust or oil from terminals and insulators will go a long way towards preventing leakage of electrical current—especially high-tension ignition current in damp or wet weather. A careful inspection of the engine compartment, from time to time, will often reveal a loose nut or clip which might allow a cable to chafe, resulting eventually in a short-circuit.

The distributor cap must be kept clean and dry, as must also the top of the *ignition coil.* Leakage of current across these surfaces is one of the most prevalent causes of difficult starting or misfiring and loss of power.

The sparking plugs will also benefit from a wipe over with a clean rag from time to time since the high-tension current may "track" across the external insulators if these are allowed to become dirty. Similarly, high-tension leads should be wiped clean. The periods at which the sparking plugs will require service will depend largely on the condition of the engine, the grade of petrol in use and the driving conditions. The practical aspects of servicing the distributor and sparking plugs are fully covered in Chapter 4.

The fan belt, which also drives the generator, should be kept free from grease and should be correctly tensioned. There should be a free movement of $\frac{1}{2}$ in. (12·7 mm) at the centre of the belt. If the belt is too slack it will not drive the fan and generator effectively. If, on the other hand, the belt is too tightly adjusted, excessive wear will occur on the fan and generator bearings. It is a simple matter to adjust the tension by loosening the two mounting bolts on the generator and the adjustment locking bolt at the front, so that the generator may be swung towards or away from the engine. It is often helpful to lever the generator gently outwards with a short length of wood by resting the end of the wood against the cylinder block. After the belt tension has been adjusted and the mounting bolts have been tightened, the free movement of the belt should then be checked.

A fairly common trouble on earlier cars is slackening-off of the dynamo bracket retaining bolts. This can be prevented by removing the bolts and coating their threads with Locktite before replacing them. A small tube of this useful preparation can be purchased from Halfords and other accessory shops.

The brakes may need more frequent adjustment when the car is driven often in traffic. The frequency at which adjustment is required will also depend on the driving methods used. The correct method of testing and adjusting the brakes is described in Chapter 6.

Starting Handle. The fact that a starting handle is not fitted to the cars is a drawback when making adjustments and when decarbonizing. Your Ford dealer can adapt the car to take a handle or the sparking plugs may be removed and the engine turned by engaging top gear and pushing the car backwards or forwards.

2 Engine decarbonizing and fault-tracing

WHEN is decarbonizing required? It is impossible to lay down any hard-and-fast rule in terms of mileage alone, since driving methods, qualities of fuel and lubricating oil used and the mechanical condition of the engine can vary so widely, and all these factors affect the rate at which carbon is deposited. In general, the need for decarbonization is indicated by progressive deterioration in performance, sometimes accompanied by a tendency of the engine to overheat and for "pinking" to occur at low speeds in top gear, together with symptoms of pre-ignition and a tendency for the engine to run-on when the ignition is switched off. These symptoms are pointers to the need for the relatively simple job involved in a systematic top overhaul of the engine.

Perhaps, at this stage, the term "pinking" should be explained. Modern premium fuels have such high octane numbers (or anti-knock properties) that "pinking," the light metallic tinkling or knocking sound heard when the engine is pulling hard, can be virtually eliminated, even though the engine may contain heavy carbon deposits. At intervals of, say, 5,000 miles (8,000 km), therefore, the level of petrol in the tank should be allowed to fall as low as is prudent and the tank should be filled with a standard grade of petrol instead of a premium fuel. Even a trace of premium fuel in the tank will tend to suppress "pinking" so it is best to use the first tankful and then to fill again with a standard petrol.

At this stage "pinking" should be evident, even in a clean engine, provided that the ignition is correctly set. It should be apparent, however, only when the engine is pulling hard in top gear and should normally become inaudible before 30 m.p.h. (50 k.p.h.) is reached. If the engine continues to "pink" at higher speeds, either the ignition is over-advanced or the combustion chambers have acquired an excessive deposit of carbon, which has raised the compression ratio of the engine.

A further point is that the presence of carbon deposits can also cause pre-ignition, owing to particles of carbon becoming incandescent and firing the mixture prematurely; that is, before the instant at which the spark normally occurs at the plug points. This will cause rough running and will aggravate "pinking." It may also cause the engine to back-fire or to run-on for several seconds after the ignition has been switched off.

It is possible to delay the point at which decarbonization is necessary by slightly retarding the ignition, as described in Chapter 4, but this should

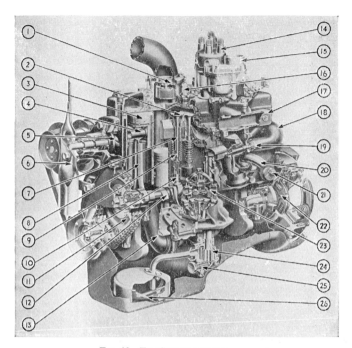

FIG. 13. THE SIDE-VALVE ENGINE

1. Thermostat	14. Ignition distributor
2. Valve	15. Carburettor
3. Piston	16. Sparking plug
4. Piston pin	17. Inlet manifold
5. Water pump impellor	18. Exhaust manifold
6. Fan	19. Exhaust control valve
7. Valve guide	20. Ventilation pipe
8. Connecting rod	21. Oil pressure warning light switch
9. Valve spring	22. Clutch disc
10. Valve tappet	23. Fuel pump
11. Timing sprocket	24. Oil pump
12. Camshaft	25. Oil relief valve
13. Crankshaft	26. Filter screen

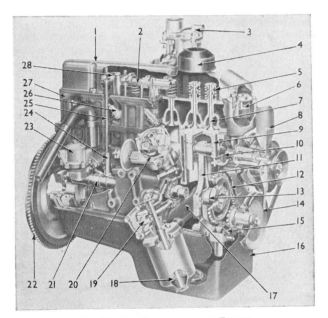

FIG. 14. THE OVERHEAD-VALVE ENGINE

1. Valve cover	15. Chain tensioner
2. Rocker shaft	16. Oil sump
3. Carburettor	17. Crankshaft
4. Oil filler	18. Oil filter
5. Valve spring	19. Oil pump
6. Thermostat	20. Ignition distributor
7. Valve	21. Camshaft
8. Fan	22. Flywheel starter ring
9. Piston	23. Petrol pump
10. Water pump	24. Tappet
11. Connecting rod	25. Push-rod
12. Timing chain	26. Sparking plug
13. Main bearing	27. Cylinder head
14. Fan driving pulley	28. Valve rocker

be regarded purely as a temporary measure. The engine should be decarbonized and the valves should be ground-in, as soon as possible.

Reduced compression in one or more cylinders can be detected by propping the throttle wide open or by asking an assistant to depress the accelerator pedal while the engine is rotated by means of the starting handle (when provided). The compression should be equal on all cylinders and each cylinder should show a distinct springy "bounce" as top-dead-centre is reached and passed. If no starting handle is available, have the compressions checked with a cylinder compression gauge. If the compression is weak on one or more cylinders the most likely cause is burnt or pitted valve faces. Leakage of gases past the piston rings cannot, of course, be discounted but this fault will normally be accompanied also by excessive oil consumption.

To conclude this brief summary of a somewhat complex subject, it should be recorded that most car manufacturers recommend that the engine of a car in the "family" class is best left undisturbed provided that it is running satisfactorily. There is little object in removing the cylinder head at any arbitrary mileage—say 10,000 miles (16,000 km)—as was once recommended, simply in order to inspect the valves and the condition of the combustion chambers. If you are in any doubt concerning the need for decarbonizing, your Ford dealer will be only too willing to advise. Should you decide to put the work in his hands, you will find that his workshop is equipped with the necessary tools to ensure a first-class job.

Carbon Formation and Removal. Rapid carbon formation is most often caused by the passage of excessive oil past the piston rings, resulting in a hard, caked deposit. In general, the hotter the surfaces, the harder the deposit, although at the exhaust valve port, heat and turbulence may result in most of the oil being burned off. An over-rich mixture also causes excessive carbon formation but this is usually of a soft, sooty nature. Where oil is leaking past piston rings, however, the products may combine with soot to form a hard coke.

Decarbonizing and valve grinding can be undertaken quite successfully by the owner, although he may have only limited experience. Before tackling the work, however, it is necessary to assemble, in addition to the usual tools used for routine maintenance, a valve spring compressor; a blunt scraper; a valve grinding tool of the rubber suction-cup type; a small tin of valve grinding paste containing both fine and coarse grades; a plentiful supply of clean rags, free from fluff; and a selection of boxes, tins or jars in which small parts can be kept, pending reassembly. A wire brush will be a useful asset and, of course, sufficient paraffin should be available to clean the various components, and a dish or tray in which to swill them. A new set of valve springs should be fitted.

It is advisable to renew all gaskets. The expense is small and is a worthwhile insurance against water or gas leakages after the engine has been

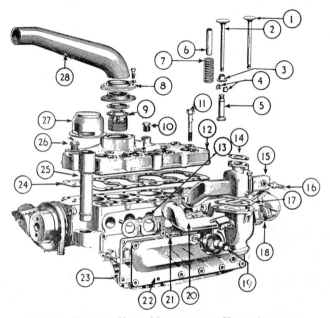

FIG. 15. CYLINDER HEAD, MANIFOLD AND VALVE ASSEMBLIES
OF SIDE-VALVE ENGINE

1. Exhaust valve
2. Inlet valve
3. Valve spring retainer
4. Split cotters
5. Valve tappet
6. Valve guide
7. Valve spring
8. Securing plate
9. Thermostat
10. Thermometer cover plug
11. Cylinder head bolt
12. Cylinder head
13. Exhaust and inlet manifold
    gasket
14. Carburettor gasket
15. Inlet manifold
16. Connector for windscreen wiper
17. Gasket
18. Exhaust control valve spring
19. Crankcase ventilation tube
20. Exhaust manifold
21. Securing nut
22. Valve chamber cover
23. Valve chamber gasket
24. Cylinder head gasket
25. Oil filler tube
26. Heater boss plug
27. Oil filler cap and breather
28. Radiator hose

reassembled, which would, of course, entail the dismantling and reassembly of the parts. The cylinder-head gasket, for example, becomes flattened and hardened in use and there is a risk of leakage if it is refitted. If a defective cylinder-head gasket allows water to leak into the cylinders, serious damage may be done to the engine. Again, although no external leakage may be apparent, gas leakage may take place between adjacent cylinders, where the gasket is narrow and is subject to relatively high gas pressure. This is a cause of misfiring and loss of power which may be difficult to diagnose.

Decarbonizing Side-valve Engine. The method of decarbonizing the side-valve engines fitted to earlier Anglias and Prefects (up to September, 1959) and to the Popular from September 1959 onwards, differs to some extent from that applying to the overhead-valve engines fitted to later Anglias and Prefects. We will deal first, therefore, with the side-valve power unit. The overhead-valve engine is covered on pages 33–7.

Dismantling. The first step is to drain the cooling system by opening the drain tap at the base of the radiator. If anti-freeze solution is to be retained for further use, a clean container, such as a two-gallon watering can, should be used. If, when the radiator tap has been opened and the cap removed, water does not flow freely, the tap should be probed with a piece of wire to dislodge any sediment.

While the water is draining, disconnect the battery cables in order to prevent the possibility of any "shorts." Disconnect the high-tension wires at the sparking plugs by pulling them off the "snap-on" terminals, and number each cable to avoid confusing them on reassembly. At this stage it is advisable to remove the sparking plugs, putting them aside for cleaning and resetting of the gaps before the engine is reassembled.

Remove the clamp and supporting strap from the air cleaner so that it can be removed. Disconnect the choke wire and throttle control rod from the carburettor.

The high-tension and low-tension wires should be disconnected from the ignition distributor. Make a note of the mark on the index scale that is opposite the indicator before removing the distributor, to facilitate timing when the distributor is refitted. Do not slacken the horizontal clamping bolt that passes through the split clamping plate beneath the distributor body. The screw that holds the distributor body clamp *to the cylinder head* should be removed and the distributor lifted.

The radiator hose may be removed after unscrewing the top clamp and bottom flange plate, after which the thermostat may be removed from the cylinder head.

Unscrew and remove the thermometer bulb, tying it back out of harm's way.

Remove the oil dipstick and breather cap, blocking the two holes with clean rag to prevent dirt or grit from entering them.

Unscrew each cylinder-head bolt a little at a time in the sequence illustrated in Fig. 16. It is important not to slacken one or more bolts completely, while the remainder are tight. The head is now free to be lifted away from the cylinder block. If it does not come away easily, no attempt should be made to prise it up by inserting a screwdriver or similar tool between the head and the block, as this may damage the machined

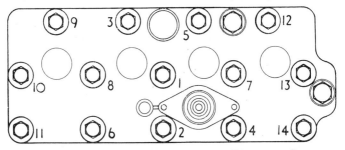

FIG. 16. CORRECT ORDER OF SLACKENING AND TIGHTENING CYLINDER HEAD BOLTS ON SIDE-VALVE ENGINES

surfaces. To free a tight cylinder head, a sharp tap with a wooden mallet or with a hammer on a block of wood held against the side of the cylinder head, should free the joint.

Typical of the Ford policy of simplification is the use of bolts instead of studs and nuts to retain the cylinder head. It is advisable to pack small strips of cloth into the tapped holes into which the retaining bolts are screwed. If carbon is allowed to accumulate in these holes it may prevent the bolts being screwed fully home when the head is refitted, causing gasket leakage and possibly serious trouble due to the passage of water past the gasket into the cylinder bores. The distributor shaft driving well and the openings in the face of the cylinder block, leading to the water spaces, should also be packed with clean rings.

Decarbonizing the Pistons. It is best to remove the carbon from the piston crowns before the valves are removed, thus preventing carbon particles or chips entering the valve guides; any possibility of accidental damage to the valve seats is also avoided.

With the starting handle, or by pulling on the fan belt, bring two of the pistons nearly to the top of the stroke and smear a little grease around the tops of these bores so that a seal is formed near the piston crown. This will prevent any particles of carbon becoming lodged between the working surfaces of the pistons and cylinder bores. Bring the pistons to the top of the stroke and stuff clean rag into the bores of the remaining two cylinders.

Remove the carbon from the piston crowns with a suitable blunt scraper. Most authorities recommend that a narrow ring of carbon should be left around the edge of the piston crown, as this ring can form a useful oil seal if the piston rings and bores are no longer in perfect condition.

Ideally, scrapers should be of softer material than the components to be cleaned. A stick of solder beaten flat at one end forms an effective

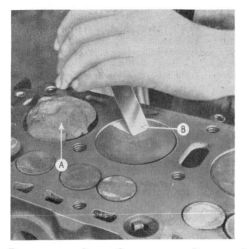

FIG. 17. DECARBONIZING PISTON CROWNS BEFORE REMOVING VALVES

Clean rag (A) should be stuffed into the open bores. A blunt scraper (B) should be employed to prevent the piston crowns being scored

scraper for the aluminium piston crowns, although bone or hardwood scrapers may be used. It must be admitted, however, that a blunted chisel or screwdriver, carefully used, is the tool most generally employed by the expert.

When two pistons have been properly cleaned, give the crankshaft a half-turn to bring the remaining pistons to the tops of their bores and deal with these two pistons in the same way. It is best to leave any deposits which may have accumulated on the face of the block in the neighbourhood of the valves until the valves are removed.

Remove the carbon from the cylinder head with a wire brush and a suitable scraper and clean the surfaces with a rag moistened with paraffin.

Scrape clean the machined surface so that it is free from rust or jointing compound and is ready for reassembly.

Removing the Valves. Having removed the carbon from the cylinder head and piston crowns, the next step is to examine the condition of the valves and valve seats. In order to do this they must be removed from the block. The first job is to detach the fuel line connexions at the carburettor and fuel pump, and the rubber tubing connecting the wiper motor to the induction pipe. The exhaust pipe clamp may now be removed so that the exhaust pipe can be disconnected from the manifold.

The carburettor and manifold may now be detached from the cylinder block by undoing the four securing nuts. The fuel pump should then be unbolted and also the crankcase ventilation tube and the oil pressure warning light lead, allowing the valve chamber plate to be removed. The two holes in the valve chamber leading to the sump should be blocked with a rag to prevent valve spring retainers or carbon particles entering them. The valves should now be removed.

If reference is made to Fig. 18 this operation should not present any real difficulty. The lower end of the compressor should be slipped under the valve spring, above the retainer, and the spring should be compressed. Remove the split taper cotters from below the spring seat, release the tension on the valve spring and remove the compressor. The spring may now be drawn clear from around the valve guide and the valve lifted from the cylinder block.

Each valve should be dealt with similarly, taking particular care to keep each valve and spring together. On no account must any of the valves be interchanged.

Note that the inlet valve heads are larger than those on the exhaust valves.

A piece of wood drilled with holes to accommodate the valve stems and numbered in sequence would be a suitable fixture for retaining them in the right order. Do not centre-punch the valve heads, as this is liable to cause distortion of the valves.

The valves, valve ports, springs and retainers should be thoroughly cleaned and the valve faces examined. The carbon deposits which could not be reached with the valves in position should now be removed.

Grinding-in the Valves. To render the valves gas-tight, it is necessary to ensure perfect contact between the bevelled surfaces of the valves and their seatings in the cylinder head. This is achieved by rotating the valves on their seatings with the aid of a wooden-handled valve grinding tool, fitted with a rubber suction cup. The grinding process consists of smearing the bevelled face of the valve with a small amount of grinding paste and lightly grinding this surface on to the valve seat in the cylinder head.

The grade of paste to be used will, of course, depend upon the condition

FIG. 18   USING VALVE SPRING COMPRESSOR TO ALLOW VALVE COTTERS
TO BE REMOVED (*above*) AND GRINDING IN VALVE WITH SUCTION TOOL
(*below*) ON SIDE-VALVE ENGINE

of the valves. If the surfaces are moderately pitted, it will be quicker to begin the grinding process with "coarse" paste until the irregular surfaces have been ground away.

If the seatings and valves are very badly pitted, however, the advice of a Ford dealer should be sought, in order that the seatings may be re-cut with special abrasive stones and the valve faces trued up in a suitable machine. Excessive grinding-in results in recessed seatings and incorrect mating angles and causes loss of power

Normal light pitting may be removed with the "fine" paste until a good matt finish has been obtained.

Before grinding the valves make sure that the camshaft is in such a position that the valve to be ground is not raised or about to be raised by the tappet; the latter should be at its lowest point to allow sufficient clearance between the foot of the valve and the adjusting screw. With a piston at the top of the compression stroke, both valves of that cylinder can be ground-in.

The valve should be rotated quickly and lightly, first in one direction and then in the other, spinning the handle of the tool between the palms of the hands. From time to time the valve should be raised from its seat and turned a quarter of a turn, grinding being continued from this new position. This will ensure that an even, concentric surface is obtained. Only a light, downward pressure on the valve is required.

When correctly ground, both the valve seat and the face of the valve should have an even, clean, grey matt finish, with no signs of bright rings or any evidence of pitting. Bright rings are caused by grinding with insufficient grinding paste, while "tramlines" are usually the result of continuously grinding the valve on its seat without taking up a different position.

A useful test to check the effectiveness of the seal is to make a series of pencil marks across the seating face of the valve with a soft lead pencil. Replace the valve and rotate it once through one complete turn on its seating. If the valve is seating properly, each pencil mark should be erased at the line of contact. If some of the lines are not broken, the indication is that either the valve or its seating is not truly circular and that renewal or re-facing of the valve or seat (or both) is required.

When all the valves have been ground-in correctly the valves and seatings should be thoroughly cleaned and all traces of grinding paste removed with a piece of clean cloth and a little petrol.

Check the valve stems and guides for wear. If they are badly worn, new valves and guides must be fitted.

Clean the valve stems and guides, lubricating the valve stems with a little clean engine oil before refitting the valves in their correct positions.

Turn the engine to bring No. 1 piston to the top of its compression stroke. At this position both valves in that cylinder are closed and their tappets are at the lowest position.

The valve springs may now be replaced around the first two valve

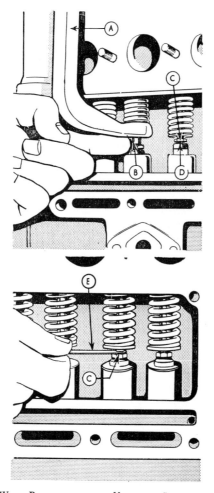

FIG. 19. WHEN REASSEMBLING THE VALVES OF SIDE-VALVE ENGINES MAKE SURE THAT THE COTTERS ARE CORRECTLY POSITIONED (*above*). THE VALVE CLEARANCE MUST THEN BE SET (*below*)

A. Valve spring compressor
B. Spring-retaining cotters
C. Self-locking tappet adjusting screw

D. Tappet
E. Feeler gauge

31

guides and the spring seat placed in position on the first valve to be assembled. Using the compressor, as shown in Fig. 19, compress the spring and fit the split cotters into the groove in the valve stem. A smear of grease on the valve stem will help to keep the cotters in position. The compressor may now be removed and the operation repeated on the other valves. Make sure, with the aid of a mirror and an inspection light, that the cotters are correctly seated in the recess around the foot of the valve stem; one cotter may have become displaced.

Checking and Adjusting Valve Clearances. It will be apparent that grinding away a small quantity of metal from the valve and seat will decrease the clearance between the foot of the valve stem and the tappet. These clearances should now be checked, using a feeler gauge as shown in Fig. 19, and should be between 0·0115 in. and 0·0135 in. (0·29–0·34 mm) when the tappet is in its lowest position.

Any adjustment necessary to bring this clearance within these limits is made on the self-locking tappet adjuster nuts. One spanner is used to hold the tappet while a second is used to screw the adjusting nut up or down as required. Each valve clearance is checked and adjusted in the same manner, turning the engine when necessary to bring each tappet on to the heel of the cam.

Reassembly. The valve chamber cover can now be replaced, using a new gasket—first making sure, of course, that the cloth blocking the holes has been removed. Note that the centre bolt in the top of the cover and the bolt nearest the fuel pump are shorter than the rest.

Replace the sump screw securing the ventilation tube bracket and connect the oil pressure warning light lead to the switch on the valve cover. Next replace the fuel pump, the flange faces of which should be clean and free of any particles of the old gasket. A new gasket must be used, since a poor joint at this point will permit considerable oil leakage and may affect the efficiency of the pump by causing distortion of the parts.

The manifold, complete with carburettor, may now be fitted, using a new gasket for the inlet manifold. Tighten the brass clamp nuts evenly and replace the fuel lines to the carburettor and fuel pump. The carburettor controls are now reconnected, the choke control being set with a slight amount of slack in the wire when the starting valve is closed and the choke knob pushed in.

Fit the windscreen wiper tube to the inlet manifold and replace the dipstick.

Replacing the Cylinder Head. Before reassembling the clean cylinder head with its new gasket, make sure that the piston crowns, cylinder walls and the top of the block are scrupulously clean. With an oil can squirt a small quantity of engine oil around each bore so that it will be distributed over the cylinder walls and down the sides of the pistons when the engine is first turned over.

The new cylinder head gasket should be smeared on both faces with high melting-point grease, and placed carefully on the block with the smooth surface downwards. Replace the cylinder head, making sure that the hole in the gasket which receives the distributor drive is in line and carefully tighten down the bolts in the order shown in Fig. 16. The air cleaner support strap fits under the bolt in front of the distributor well and, where an engine earth strap is fitted, this is secured by the bolt at the centre of the rear edge of the head.

Distortion of the head can be avoided by first tightening the centre nut and working outwards toward the extremities. Screw each nut right down by hand first and then give each a half-turn with a spanner, following this up with a whole turn until each is tight: it is not necessary to use excessive force.

Final Stages. Refit the distributor, being careful to see that the tongue on the distributor shaft is located correctly in the slot provided on the drive shaft. As the slot is machined off-centre, there is little risk of installing the distributor incorrectly. Set the graduated index scale arm to its original position.

Unless the sparking plugs are fairly new, fit a new set. Reconnect the high-tension wires to the plugs and also the high- and low-tension wires to the coil Replace the radiator hose and thermostat, and screw the thermometer bulb securely home. Do not forget the breather cap. Replace the air cleaner with gauze end to the front of the engine.

Refill the radiator, check the oil level in the sump and start up. After allowing the engine to get well warmed up, switch off and go over the cylinder head and manifold nuts again. The nuts should be checked a second time after about 300 miles (about 500 km) running.

When the engine has been decarbonized the ignition timing should be checked as described in Chapter 4. It is usually possible to advance the ignition slightly. Also, the carburettor slow-running mixture strength and speed will usually require readjustment. These attentions will improve the performance and fuel economy of the engine and will ensure that the maximum benefit is obtained from the "top overhaul."

DECARBONIZING OVERHEAD-VALVE ENGINES

Much of what has already been said applies also, in general terms, to the overhead-valve engines. The method of dismantling these engines differs, however, owing to the fact that the valve gear is carried on the cylinder head. This complicates dismantling to some extent but, on the other hand, renders the removal and grinding-in of the valves a somewhat simpler job, as this can be done with the cylinder head on the bench. It is proposed, therefore, to cover only essential differences between the two types of engines, the remainder of the information already given in this chapter being common to both designs.

Removing the Cylinder Head. The cooling system is drained by opening the two taps, one fitted beneath the centre of the radiator and the other adjacent to the generator on the left-hand side of the engine. The sparking plug leads are disconnected by pulling them off the snap-on terminals. Each wire should be numbered as it is removed in order to avoid any possibility of confusion on reassembly. The sparking plugs should be taken out and set aside for cleaning and gapping, although it is better to fit a new set when the engine is reassembled. After the air cleaner has been removed from the carburettor, unscrew the hose clip and remove the hose from the cylinder-head water outlet. Disconnect the heater water inlet hose if a heater is fitted. The vacuum ignition control pipe should be disconnected at the union on the carburettor, and the fuel pipe union uncoupled. When the carburettor controls have been disconnected the carburettor should be removed from the inlet manifold. Disconnect the exhaust manifold from the silencer pipe by unscrewing the clamp.

Take off the valve rocker cover, unscrew the rocker shaft retaining bolts and remove the rocker shaft assembly. The push rods should then be lifted vertically, giving each a twist to break the oil suction between its base and the tappet, and should be laid aside in the order in which they are removed, since each rod becomes lapped to its tappet and rocker.

The cylinder head bolts can now be unscrewed in the reverse order to that shown in Fig. 20, leaving the head free to be lifted away. If it appears to be tight, give it a sharp tap with a wooden mallet or with a hammer, interposing a block of wood between the side of the head and the hammer.

The head can now be taken to the bench for decarbonizing. It is best to remove the carbon from the combustion chambers before taking out the valves, in order to avoid any risk of damaging the valve seatings. The piston crowns and the upper surface of the cylinder block can be cleaned as previously described, care being taken to prevent the entry of carbon into the tapped holes in the cylinder block gasket face, which might prevent the bolts being fully tightened down when the engine is reassembled.

Returning to the cylinder head, a valve spring compressor should be used to compress each spring, allowing the tapered retaining collets to be removed. Take off the spring retainer, the spring and the umbrella-type oil seal. The valve may then be withdrawn from the cylinder head. As each valve is removed it should be placed in order so that it will be returned to its correct seating. It is a wise plan to push the stems through holes in a sheet of cardboard, numbered to correspond with the positions of the valves in the engine. It is not advisable to centre-punch the valve heads in order to identify them, as this is liable to cause distortion of the valves. It will be noticed that the inlet valve heads are of larger diameter than those of the exhaust valves.

With the valves out of the way, the carbon can be scraped out of the exhaust ports and the inlet ports also cleaned up. When the cylinder head is thoroughly clean, and any doubtful valves have been renewed, the valves should be lightly ground into their seatings, using the technique described earlier in this chapter. The valves should then be reassembled, preferably installing new valve springs. See that the oil seals are correctly fitted and

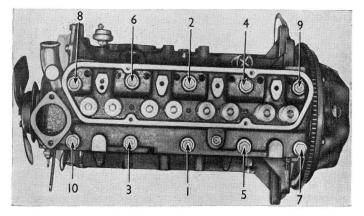

FIG. 20. THE CYLINDER-HEAD BOLTS OF OVERHEAD-VALVE ENGINES
SHOULD BE TIGHTENED PROGRESSIVELY IN THE ORDER SHOWN

that the retaining collets are installed snugly in their grooves. The application of a little grease to the collets will facilitate assembly.

Be careful to clean every trace of carbon out of the bolt-holes in the cylinder block before refitting the cylinder head. Otherwise the bolts may "bottom" in the holes before compressing the cylinder-head gasket sufficiently to provide a sound joint. Repeated gasket failures can usually be traced to this fault, but remember that gasket leakage can also be caused by a warped cylinder head or, less usually, a distorted cylinder block. A Ford dealer should be able to true-up either surface satisfactorily. The most logical plan is to take the cylinder head to him for checking, in the hope that the trouble will be confined to this component.

When fitting the new cylinder head gasket, smear both sides with grease and carefully lower the cylinder head into place. Replace the cylinder-head bolts and tighten each down until it is finger tight before applying the final tightening pressure in the order shown in Fig. 20.

The valve gear can then be reassembled, making sure that each push-rod fits correctly into the recess in its tappet and that the ball-ended adjusting screw is correctly located in the cup at the top of the rod. The rocker shaft bolts can then be tightened down carefully and the valve clearance adjusted as described below.

Adjusting Valve Clearances on Overhead-valve Engines. If you are to get the best from an overhead-valve Anglia, it will pay to take particular

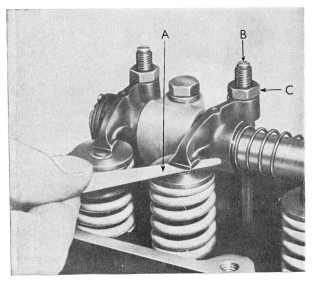

FIG. 21. ADJUSTING THE ROCKER CLEARANCE

A. Feeler gauge   *C.* Lock-nut
B. Adjusting screw

care in adjusting the valve clearances—certainly to aim at being within 0·001 in. (0·025 mm) of the recommended clearance given in Chapter 8. This will probably entail rechecking each clearance after rotating the engine once or twice, but the trouble will be well worthwhile.

To adjust the clearances, slacken the lock-nut on the adjusting screw and turn the latter clockwise to reduce the clearance and anti-clockwise in order to increase it. The blade of a feeler gauge must be inserted between the tip of the valve stem and the face of the rocker, as shown in Fig. 21. When the gap is correctly adjusted, there should be a slight drag on the feeler gauge as it is withdrawn. As this adjustment is carried out with the engine cold, the clearances should be re-checked when reassembly has been completed and the engine has been run until it reaches its normal operating temperature.

In order to ensure that each valve is fully closed, check as follows—

Valves Open	Valves to Adjust
1 and 6	3 and 8
3 and 8	1 and 6
2 and 4	5 and 7
5 and 7	2 and 4

Exhaust valves, Nos. 1, 4, 5 and 8
Inlet valves, Nos. 2, 3, 6 and 7

Two points should be borne in mind when adjusting overhead valve clearances. First, the clearance should be checked only when the engine has been run for a sufficiently long period to allow all the components to reach their normal working temperature. If the clearances are measured when the engine has been running for only a few minutes, a misleading figure will be obtained. Secondly, the clearance must be rechecked whenever the cylinder-head bolts are tightened down, as tightening the bolts results in compression of the gasket, which in turn moves the cylinder head downwards in relation to the push-rods and decreases the effective valve clearance. It will be necessary to tighten down the cylinder-head bolts and check the valve clearances, therefore, after the engine has covered 200–300 miles (400–500 km) after an overhaul, to compensate for the initial settling-down of the cylinder-head gasket.

ENGINE STARTING TROUBLES

Starter Motor Faults

Starter motor does not turn engine	*Probable Fault* Battery discharged or worn out. Battery connections or earthing strap loose or corroded. Faulty starter switch. Dirty starter drive. Drive spring broken. Faulty starter motor. Engine water pump frozen.
Turns Engine Slowly	*Probable Fault* Battery partly discharged or nearing end of life. Battery connections or earthing strap loose or corroded. Too heavy a grade of engine oil in use. Faulty starter motor.
Starter operates but Pinion will not engage with Flywheel Ring	Dirt or excessive wear on pinion drive, preventing the control nut running along the screwed sleeve. Removal of the starter, cleaning the drive and renewal of any worn parts will usually cure the trouble. Low battery voltage is also a possible cause. When a pre-engaged starter is fitted, check the solenoid-operated engagement mechanism.
Pinion will not disengage If the pinion is jammed in mesh with the flywheel ring gear, a click will be heard from the starter solenoid switch when the key switch is turned. To free the pinion, see page 76.	Dirt or grit on pinion sleeve. Badly worn or damaged teeth on pinion or on flywheel gear.
	Excessively Noisy Starter Loose starter mounting bolts or worn or damaged pinion or flywheel ring gear.

ENGINE STARTING TROUBLES (*contd.*)

Engine Will Not Fire

Carry out the following checks in sequence (see text)

IGNITION SYSTEM	FUEL SYSTEM
Battery Check	**Fuel System Check**
Switch on lights and check brightness when starter is operated.	Check that petrol reaches carburettor when engine is rotated by starter, by disconnecting pipe at carburettor.
Lamps do not light, or are weak— *Probable Fault*	No petrol reaching carburettor— *Probable Fault*
Battery discharged (*see also* pages 67 and 71).	Petrol tank empty.
Battery connections or earthing strap loose or corroded.	Choked petrol filter.
Faulty ignition switch.	Air-leak in pipeline.
Lights dim only slightly—	Faulty petrol pump.
Loose connection or broken wire between switch and ignition coil or distributor.	Air vent to tank clogged.
	Blockage in pipeline.
Sparking Plug Check	Petrol reaching Carburettor
Remove a plug, reconnect the lead and lay the plug on the cylinder block. Watch for sparks while the engine is rotated.	Mixture too rich or too weak.
No spark at plug gap—	Water in petrol.
Condensed moisture on distributor cap or plug leads or insulators.	Jet obstructed.
Oil or condensed fuel or water on plug points or internal insulator.	Bad air leak in induction manifold or air carburettor flange.
Sparking plug internal or external insulator dirty or cracked.	
Ignition system trouble (*see below*)	
Ignition Distributor Check	**OTHER POSSIBLE CAUSES OF DIFFICULT STARTING**
Remove sparking plug lead from plug, hold bare end of lead ⅜ in. from unpainted metal of engine. Rotate engine with ignition switched on.	Broken distributor drive.
No spark from sparking plug lead—	Timing chain broken or has jumped sprocket teeth.
Contact-breaker points dirty or pitted, or not opening and closing.	Exhaust tailpipe blocked.
Cracked rotor.	
Poor connections in low-tension circuit.	
Faulty distributor cap.	
Faulty condenser or connections.	
Spring contact blade on rotor bent or broken.	
Coil burnt out.	
Spark from plug lead—	
Trouble must lie in sparking plugs.	

39

MISCELLANEOUS ENGINE TROUBLES

SYMPTOM	PROBABLE CAUSE		
	Ignition	*Fuel system*	*Other Faults*
Misfiring	Incorrect gap at sparking-plug points. Dirty or cracked sparking-plug insulators. Wrong type of sparking plugs. Damp or oily deposits on high-tension leads, sparking-plug, distributor or coil insulation. High-tension or low-tension leads loose or short-circuiting. Faulty ignition interference suppressors if fitted).	Water in carburettor. Petrol pipe partly blocked. Fuel pump pressure low. Fuel pump filter choked. Carburettor needle valve faulty or dirty. Jet obstructed.	Incorrect valve clearance. Valve sticking. Valve seatings burnt. Valve spring broken. Leaking cylinder head-gasket
Engine Fires but Will Not Continue to Run	Condensation on plug points. Low-tension connection loose. Broken wire in distributor between capacitor and contact-breaker points. Faulty ignition switch-contact. Contact-breaker rocker arm sticking. Dirty contact-breaker points.	Carburettor needle valve sticking. Fuel pump faulty. Petrol pipe partly blocked. Jet obstructed. Water in petrol.	Exhaust tailpipe obstructed. Incorrect ignition or valve timing
Engine Runs on Wide Throttle Opening Only		Slow-running mixture strength and/or idling speed incorrect. Jet obstructed. Air leak at carburettor or inlet manifold flange.	Valves sticking. Valve seatings burnt. Valve spring broken.
Engine Does not Give Full Power	Ignition timing retarded. Ignition timing over-advanced. Ignition faults (*see* under *Misfiring*).	Petrol supply troubles (*see* above). Throttle not opening fully. Jet obstructed. Carburettors need synchronizing (tuned engines only).	Incorrect valve clearances. Valve seating burnt. Partial engine seizure—(*see Overheating*). Leaking cylinder-head gasket. Low compression due to worn piston rings and cylinders.

MISCELLANEOUS ENGINE TROUBLES (contd.)

SYMPTOM	PROBABLE CAUSE		
	Ignition	*Fuel System*	*Other Faults*
Overheating	Ignition timing incorrect—too far advanced or retarded. Wrong type of sparking plug overheating and causing pre-ignition.	Weak mixture (see under *Misfiring*).	Filler cap not retaining pressure in cooling system. Too little water in radiator. Fan belt slipping or broken. Choked radiator (water and air passages). Lime and rust deposits in cooling system. Perished or collapsed water hoses. Faulty thermostat. Leaking cylinder-head gasket. Too little oil in engine. Tight engine after overhaul.
Knocking or Pinking	Ignition timing too far advanced. Wrong type of sparking plugs fitted, overheating and causing pre-ignition.	Wrong grade of fuel in use—use premium grade. If this does not cure trouble, check for faults listed in other columns.	Excessive carbon deposit or badly-seating valves—engine needs top-overhaul. Worn bearings, pistons or other mechanical faults.

3 Fuel system and carburettor

WHEN difficult starting, misfiring and loss of power are experienced the average owner is often apt to blame the carburettor. Experience has shown, however, that only in comparatively few cases is the carburettor or the fuel system at fault. The trouble may be due to a combination of other faults, such as ignition system troubles, badly seating valves, worn piston rings and cylinders, leaking cylinder-head gaskets, defective inlet manifold or carburettor gaskets, and mechanical faults, such as binding brakes. All these troubles can adversely affect performance and fuel consumption and some of them can contribute very substantially to difficult starting.

Before blaming the carburettor, therefore, a general check should be made on the mechanical condition of the engine and the car as a whole. Your authorized Ford dealer has the necessary equipment to carry out such checks quickly and efficiently. It should not be necessary to stress the value of expert opinion in cases of this nature and when discussing faults such as difficult starting and excessive fuel consumption in this chapter it will be assumed that these preliminary checks have been carried out.

If the simple maintenance described in this chapter is conscientiously carried out, however, carburettor and fuel system faults should seldom be experienced. It should be emphasized that the carburettor itself does not "wear out" in the general sense of the word during the normal life of a car. Apart from the throttle spindle bearings there are virtually no wearing parts in the carburettor in the accepted sense.

THE CARBURETTOR

Fuel is fed from the rear tank by a mechanical petrol pump which is driven from the engine camshaft and which supplies the down-draught carburettor. Although the carburettor might appear to be a some-what complex instrument it is, in fact, quite straighforward and well within the scope of the average owner to maintain.

Settings that differ from standard will, however, be necessary in countries in which there is any marked difference in the type of petrol available, in atmospheric conditions or in the altitudes at which the car is normally operated. In such cases the advice of the local Ford agent should be sought if the performance of the car indicates that an alteration in the

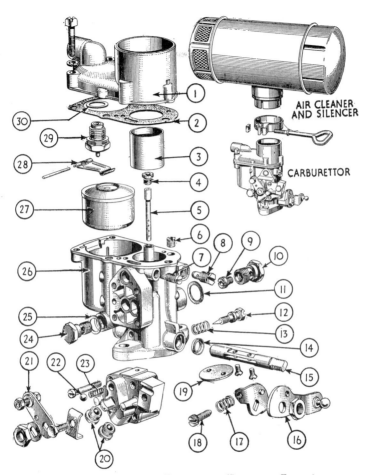

FIG. 22. DOWNDRAUGHT CARBURETTOR (SIDE-VALVE ENGINE)

1. Float-chamber cover
2. Gasket
3. Choke tube
4. Main air correction jet
5. Emulsion tube
6. Auxiliary air bleed jet
7. Choke securing screw
8. Slow-running jet
9. Main jet
10. Main jet carrier bolt
11. Washer

12. Volume control screw
13. Spring
14. Throttle spindle gland
15. Throttle spindle
16. Carburettor throttle lever
17. Spring
18. Idling adjustment screw
19. Throttle plate
20. Starting carburettor air jets

21. Starting control
22. Locating ball
23. Spring
24. Starter petrol jet
25. Washer
26. Carburettor body
27. Float
28. Float lever
29. Needle valve assembly
30. Washer

size of jets fitted is necessary. The settings quoted in Chapter 8 are intended as a general guide when expert advice is not available.

Carburettor Adjustment. The throttle stop screw controls the amount by which the throttle approaches the closed position and therefore regulates the slow-running speed. The richness of the slow-running mixture is determined by the volume control screw, a greater volume of mixture being admitted, and the mixture enriched, when the screw is turned anticlockwise.

To obtain the exact settings the engine should be at normal running temperature and the throttle stop screw turned so that the engine will run just fast enough to prevent stalling. The volume adjusting screw should then be screwed in or out until the engine runs evenly. The throttle stop screw should now be readjusted if the engine is running too fast, followed by a further adjustment of the volume adjusting screw. The operations should be repeated until satisfactory idling is obtained.

Turning the volume control screw in an anti-clockwise direction provides a richer mixture. If the mixture is too rich, the engine runs with a rhythmic beat and the exhaust may show dark smoke. If the mixture is too weak, the engine is likely to stall when suddenly accelerated and the exhaust will sound irregular and "splashy."

The strength of the slow-running mixture considerably influences acceleration from low speeds. If there is a "flat spot" when the throttle is opened from the idling position, try the effect of slightly enriching the slow-running mixture; half-a-turn of the screw may be sufficient. It will probably be necessary to adjust the stop screw slightly to prevent "lumpy" idling, but an idling setting that is slightly on the rich side is an advantage.

Remember that it will be impossible to obtain good idling if ignition or mechanical faults exist—a subject that has already been mentioned at the beginning of the chapter.

Starting Carburettor. This is fitted to earlier carburettors (Figs. 22 and 23). It is virtually a small, self-contained caburettor built into the main unit and drawing its petrol supply from the main float chamber. The component parts can be seen in Fig. 22.

To start the engine from cold a very rich mixture is required. When the dashboard "choke" knob is pulled out the throttle should not be opened by depressing the throttle pedal as this will destroy the suction created at the outlet from the starting carburettor; this carburettor is so designed that normal starting should take place with the throttle in the normal idling position.

When the choke control knob is pulled out, two control valves in the starting carburettor are opened, allowing a balanced mixture of petrol and air to be drawn into the induction system from below the throttle. This mixture is weakened when the engine picks up and runs, so that the detrimental effects of an over-rich mixture are avoided.

When the engine is running and the throttle is opened the mixture provided by the starting carburettor supplements that from the normal jets. The intermediate position of the control will enable the cold engine to pull satisfactorily during the warming-up period. Once the engine has

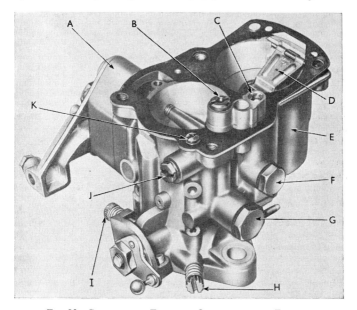

FIG. 23. CARBURETTOR FITTED TO OVERHEAD-VALVE ENGINES
EXCEPT LATER ANGLIA AND ANGLIA SUPER

A. Starting carburettor
B. Main air bleed
C. Economizer jet air bleed
D. Float lever
E. Float chamber
F. Economizer jet

G. Main jet
H. Idling mixture adjustment
I. Idling speed adjustment
J. Idling jet
K. Idling jet air bleed

become warm and the choke control is pushed fully home, the starting carburettor is put out of action.

It will be seen that the only faults likely to cause trouble are incorrect adjustment of the wire from the dashboard control to the starting carburettor or blockage of the starting carburettor jet. In each case the remedy is obvious. Where the control wire is concerned, this should be clamped so that there is a slight free movement of the dashboard control before the slack is taken up; on the other hand, if too much free movement is permitted the control valve may not be fully opened when the choke control is operated.

On the type of carburettor fitted to later models (Fig. 24), however, the rich starting mixture is provided by a semi-automatic strangler or choke flap in the air intake. If difficulty is experienced in starting, therefore, check first that the choke control wire is correctly adjusted and then remove the air cleaner and make sure that the strangler flap itself closes fully when the control is operated.

This type of carburettor incorporates an accelerator pump which injects a spurt of fuel whenever the accelerator pedal is depressed. In very cold weather it may help to pump the accelerator once or twice, but it is only too easy to inject too much fuel by doing this, thus producing an over-rich mixture which will make it impossible to start the engine, especially when it is warm. To cure this, depress the accelerator pedal fully and hold the throttle wide open while rotating the engine with the starter motor. The choke control should, of course, be pushed fully home during this process.

Difficult Starting. It should not be assumed that the carburettor is necessarily to blame when difficult starting is experienced. Ignition faults are among the most likely causes of this trouble and the ignition system should be systematically checked over as described in Chapter 4. Similarly, the condition of the piston rings and of the engine generally can considerably influence the ease of starting in very cold weather, although such faults may be of relatively little importance during the summer months. Finally, a weak battery or an inefficient starter motor, which fails to rotate the engine at a sufficiently high cranking speed, can render it very difficult indeed to obtain the conditions within the combustion chambers that are necessary to ensure an easy start.

As far as the carburettor is concerned, therefore, attention should be limited to checking the adjustment of the starting carburettor control and cleaning the jets. It should also be verified that the float-chamber cover retaining bolts are firmly tightened.

It should be remembered that if the engine has previously started satisfactorily—which will undoubtedly be the case with a new engine or one which has been reconditioned—then the onset of starting troubles cannot be attributed to the necessity of altering the existing jets or settings. Only if the jets have been tampered with by another owner or by the present owner of the car, should it be necessary to alter them. Except in the circumstances already referred to earlier in this chapter, the standard setting should be restored, when no further difficulty should be experienced.

Cleaning the Jets. If the engine cannot be made to tick-over for any length of time or stalls when decelerating, the slow-running jet may be blocked. Water or foreign matter may enter the float chamber and be drawn into the jet, causing erratic running or complete loss of power. The main, compensating and slow-running jets should, therefore, be removed occasionally for cleaning.

The slow-running, main, economy and starter jets can all be removed without dismantling the carburettor. Jets should be cleaned by washing them in petrol and blowing through them in the reverse direction to the normal flow of fuel. Never use wire to probe the jets. They are calibrated to very fine limits and engine performance and economy will suffer if these jet orifices are altered. The jets are clearly numbered—the greater the number the larger the jet.

After cleaning the jets the slow-running adjustments should, if necessary, be reset.

Float-chamber and Float. The opportunity should be taken when cleaning the jets to clean out the float bowl. This can best be done by swilling it out with petrol to ensure that all sediment has been removed. The two screws securing the float-chamber cover should be removed and the cover lifted off to gain access to the float-chamber.

Flooding, on the other hand, can usually be attributed to the presence of dirt or grit in the needle valve assembly although it may possibly be caused by a punctured float. A quick check for the latter trouble is to immerse the float in boiling water, when bubbles will reveal the location of any pinholes. Immediately bubbling has ceased, the puncture may be sealed with a trace of solder. This should be considered as a temporary repair only, since the extra weight of even a spot of solder may cause a difference in petrol level in the bowl. A new float should be fitted at the earliest opportunity.

Excessive Fuel Consumption. Flooding or too high a petrol level in the float chamber is, of course, one of the most likely causes of excessive fuel consumption. Leakage at any of the joints on the carburettor can also increase fuel consumption by a significant figure. Usually, however, the carburettor is blamed for heavy fuel consumption when the trouble is in fact due to poor mechanical condition of the engine or to ignition faults, such as dirty sparking plugs, incorrectly set plug gaps, dirty or pitted contact-breaker points, or over-retarded ignition timing. Binding brakes are another common cause. Moreover, short journeys and town driving increase the petrol consumption. The average figure is generally stated by car manufacturers in terms of country running over give-and-take roads with normal loads, at a speed of between 30 and 35 m.p.h., but the actual consumption may vary between 32 and over 40 m.p.g., depending on conditions and driving methods.

Higher fuel consumption than normal is also likely to occur if the choke control does not have a little free movement when in the closed position, with the result that the engine, as it rocks on its mountings, operates the choke lever on the carburettor.

If, however, the consumption is considered to be too high when the carburettor, ignition system and engine are in good mechanical condition and correctly adjusted the owner who values economy above performance can try the effect of fitting a main jet one size smaller. A road test may show that although mileage per gallon has increased, power has fallen off. To rectify this, a smaller air correction jet may be fitted to enrich the mixture at higher engine speeds.

A less likely cause of excessive fuel consumption is the generation of too high a pressure by the fuel pump. This is usually indicated by the fact that it is impossible to obtain a really smooth tick-over, whatever the position of the air-adjusting screw. Black smoke will be apparent from the exhaust and when running downhill with the throttle partly closed petrol fumes may be apparent in the car.

In order to overcome this trouble it will be necessary to fit a slightly smaller needle seating to the carburettor in order to control the excessive pressure. Your Ford agent or dealer will be able to advise you on this point. If this does not cure the trouble, it may be necessary to fit a thicker packing between the petrol pump and the flange on the crankcase.

Lack of Power and Poor Acceleration. The acceleration is controlled principally by the size of the main and correction jets and the adjustment of the slow-running screw. If acceleration is poor, therefore, on all models except the first series of the overhead-valve Anglia (about which more will be said in a moment) the jets should be removed and cleaned and the slow-running volume adjustment should be set so that the mixture is slightly on the rich side, rather than slightly "lean." It should be emphasized that it should not be necessary to change the size of the jets if the car has previously been behaving normally. If, however, a slightly better performance than standard is required the effect of a size larger main jet and a larger correction jet can be tried; naturally, if the increased performance is used, some deterioration in fuel consumption must be expected.

With the latest type of carburettor fitted with an accelerator pump, poor acceleration—in fact, a pronounced "flat spot"—will occur if the pump jet becomes blocked or if the pump does not operate for any reason. If you suspect that this is the case, it would be as well to have a word with a Ford dealer.

Again it must be emphasized, however, that lack of power is more likely to be due to dirty or incorrectly adjusted plugs than to carburettor faults. Similarly if the compression is poor as a result of worn piston rings and cylinders or leaking valves, the engine will not pull well although it may behave reasonably satisfactorily when running at fairly high speeds on small throttle openings.

Possible exceptions to the general rules just mentioned are the first 49,527 overhead-valve Anglias on which the carburettors originally fitted caused a pronounced flat spot during acceleration. The Ford Motor

Company modified the carburettor to cure the trouble and offered, as a free service, to exchange the existing carburettor for the modified unit, which transforms the performance and smoothness of the car at low speeds. If your engine number is below 49,528, therefore, and you have reason to believe that the change has not been carried out, it would be well worth while consulting a Ford dealer.

Maximum speed is controlled by the main jet and here again a one size larger main jet can be tried if it is desired to increase the speed—a step which would normally not be contemplated by the average owner, since the car is not designed for very high maximum speeds but rather for reasonable cruising speeds and a high degree of economy. In fact, if it is desired to tune the engine, consult a specialist tuning firm. It is seldom satisfactory to attempt to obtain any considerable increase in performance by minor alterations to the carburation and ignition settings.

Carburettor Air Cleaner. The mileage at which the air cleaner needs attention will depend, of course, on the conditions under which the car is driven. In dusty conditions it will need more frequent attention, but 5,000 miles (8,000 km) is normally the maximum mileage at which the air cleaner should be serviced.

The standard gauze type of filter unit is removed by slackening the clamp securing it to the carburettor and releasing the support strap to the cylinder head. Immerse the gauze end in petrol and wash thoroughly. Allow to dry, dip the gauze in clean engine oil and shake off the surplus oil. The later type of gauze filter is cleaned by pouring petrol into it through the larger-diameter hole, swilling it round and emptying it through the "spout." The element should then be lightly oiled in the same way, allowing surplus oil to drain off before refitting the cleaner. Refit with the gauze end towards the front of the car.

The oil-bath type air cleaner, which is fitted to certain models, can be cleaned by unscrewing the wing nut on the top cover and lifting the top and filter unit from the body of the filter. Empty the oil and clean out any accumulation of sludge. The filter should be washed in petrol and the air cleaner body filled with fresh engine oil up to the level of the arrow.

PETROL PUMP

The petrol pump is entirely automatic in action. Little attention should be needed other than to keep the filter free from dirt and sediment. An occasional check should be made to ensure that the fuel pipe unions are tight.

The method of operation applies equally to the petrol pump section of the combined petrol and vacuum pump fitted to the later Prefect engines (*see* page 52). The rocker arm is held by a spring in permanent contact with an eccentric on the engine camshaft. As the camshaft revolves, the rocker arm moves back and draws the pull rod and diaphragm downwards against the pressure of the return spring, thus creating a vacuum in the pump chamber in the upper casting, above the diaphragm.

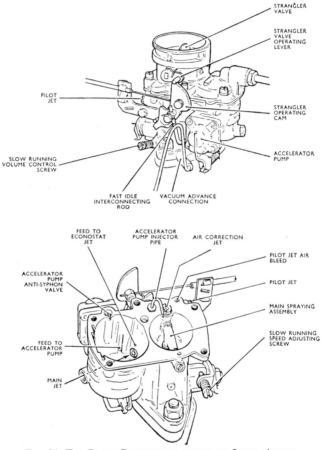

Fig. 24. The Solex Carburettor fitted to Later Anglia and Anglia Super

Petrol from the tank enters the sediment chamber, passes through the filter gauze and then past the inlet valve into the pump chamber. On the return stroke, pressure exerted by the spring pushes the diaphragm upwards, forcing the petrol from the chamber through the outlet valve and into the carburettor feed pipe.

When the carburettor float-chamber is filled to the correct level, its float will close the inlet needle valve, thus interrupting the flow of fuel and creating a pressure in the pump chamber which is sufficient to prevent movement of the diaphragm. The cessation of diaphragm movement under these conditions is possible because the rocker arm is formed in two sections, the outer section operating the inner one by a stop incorporated at a point above the rocker-arm pin. The movement induced by the cam is absorbed by the "break" in the rocker arm whenever additional petrol is not required in the carburettor.

Pump Failure. No attempt should be made to dismantle the pump if it fails to operate. Your Ford dealer or agent will be able to supply and fit a reconditioned, guaranteed pump in exchange for the faulty unit. The notes which follow, therefore, are intended only for owners who are unable to take advantage of the specialized Ford service. It must be emphasized that, normally, petrol and vacuum pumps are dismantled and reassembled only with the aid of special equipment and should be tested after reassembly to verify that the pump is delivering the correct quantity of fuel and is developing the correct pressure.

If the test equipment is not available, a comparatively simple test of fuel delivery can be carried out by disconnecting the fuel feed pipe from the carburettor and having an assistant turn the engine by means of the starter motor. A distinct spurt of petrol should be evident for each two revolutions of the engine. If insufficient petrol is reaching the carburettor, first check that there is sufficient fuel in the tank and that the filter screen and sediment chamber are not choked with sediment. Secondly, check the connexions in the fuel pipe from the pump to the tank for air leaks, which will result in air being drawn into the system and so prevent the pump being primed.

If, when these points have been attended to, the pump still does not deliver sufficient petrol, the cause of the trouble will probably lie in the pump valves. In order to inspect these it is necessary to remove the pump from the crankcase, after first disconnecting the petrol inlet and outlet pipe unions and undoing the two studs securing the pump to the cylinder block. After turning off the fuel tap or plugging the tank pipeline as described on page 12 to prevent leakage of petrol from the pipe, the pump can be taken to the bench for dismantling.

In order to obtain access to the valves the top casting must be removed from the body of the pump. The edges of the two flanges should be lightly marked to facilitate reassembly, before the securing screws are removed. Carefully separate the diaphragm from the upper flange and do not disturb it or any part of the operating linkage.

The valves and valve springs can then be removed by undoing the two screws. On later pumps the valves, springs, and seatings are caged assemblies. The low cost of these parts enables them to be replaced as a matter of routine (unless in perfect condition) and their renewal as a whole is unquestionably the best and safest procedure. This applies also to the diaphragm and pull rod assembly, which can be removed by rotating the diaphragm through 90 degrees to disengage the pull rod from the inner rocking arm.

Before the top casting (with the valves reassembled) is refitted to the lower part of the pump the diaphragm must be fully flexed. This is the most important operation in fuel and vacuum pump service. Insufficient flexing of the diaphragm reduces the efficiency of the pump. In extreme cases the diaphragm may be torn.

The pump diaphragm should be flexed as follows. The rocker arm should be pushed towards the pump until the diaphragm is level with the body flange. Place the upper half of the pump in the correct position as shown by the marks made on the edges of the flanges. Replace the cover screws and lock washers and tighten them until the heads of the screws just engage the washers. Release the rocker arm, which will allow the diaphragm to rise to its highest position. Tighten the screws fully.

The edges of the diaphragm should now be about flush with the two clamping flanges. Any appreciable protrusion of the diaphragm indicates incorrect fitting.

The pump is now ready for testing and should first be flushed by immersing it in paraffin and working the rocker arm half-a-dozen times. The pump should then be emptied by continuing to operate the rocker arm while holding the pump above the paraffin bath. A finger should then be placed over the inlet union and the rocker operated several times On removing the finger, a distinct noise should be heard, denoting that the pump has developed a reasonable degree of suction. Now place the finger over the outlet union and press the rocker arm inwards; the air drawn into the pump chamber should be held under compression for two or three seconds. This test should be repeated with the pump immersed in paraffin and the clamping flange of the diaphragm watched carefully for any sign of air leakage.

Combined Fuel and Vacuum Pump. On later Prefect engines, a combined fuel feed and vacuum pump is fitted, the vacuum section providing a more constant depression to operate the windscreen wiper than is available with the simpler arrangement of a reserve-vacuum tank used on other cars. The vacuum pump itself requires no maintenance and if the combined pump unit develops trouble it is as well to enlist the aid of a Ford dealer, since it is of more complicated construction than the straightforward petrol pump just described.

4 The ignition system

THE experience of the road patrols operated by the Royal Automobile Club and the Automobile Association has shown that the great majority of roadside breakdowns are caused by ignition system faults. This is understandable in view of the fact that the ignition system contains a number of components which are relatively easily put out of action if they are not maintained satisfactorily. On the other hand, the actual work involved in maintenance is simplicity itself and any practical-minded owner should experience no difficulty in keeping the ignition system in first-class condition. The time spent will be more than repaid by enhanced performance, better fuel consumption and trouble-free starting during the winter months.

The ignition system is of the battery-and-coil type, consisting of an ignition coil which draws its current from the car battery and which contains two windings. One, the primary winding—a relatively heavy winding consisting of a few hundred turns—carries the battery current. Whenever the contact-breaker points open, the current flowing through this primary winding is interrupted and a surge of high-voltage current is set up in the secondary winding, which consists of many thousands of turns of fine wire and is wound beneath the primary winding, around the iron core of the ignition coil.

The surge of high-voltage current, which may amount to twenty thousand volts or more, passes from the central terminal of the ignition coil to the central terminal on the distributor cap. From this point it travels down through a spring-loaded brush or contact to the rotating distributor rotor, which passes in turn each of four electrodes within the distributor cap. Each electrode is connected to a sparking plug through the sparking plug lead, the sequence being that appropriate to the firing order of the engine—i.e. 1, 2, 4, 3. It is worth mentioning that this order differs from the more usual firing order (1, 3, 4, 2) used on the majority of other four-cylinder engines.

When the pulse of current reaches the central electrode of the sparking plug it has no option but to jump across the gap between the central electrode and the side electrode, which is, of course, "earthed" through the body of the sparking plug to the metal of the engine. To say that the current has no option but to jump the gap assumes, of course, that both the internal and the external insulators of the sparking plug are clean and in good condition; otherwise the current can leak across one of these insulators to the metal of the plug body without jumping the gap.

Without going into technicalities, it will be seen that the efficiency of the ignition system depends on good connexions at the battery terminals and the low-tension terminals on the coil, and on the high-tension connexions at the top of the coil and the centre of the distributor cap—and also on the condition of those vital items, the contact-breaker points, within the distributor itself. If these points are burnt or badly pitted the flow of current through them will be insufficient to generate a satisfactory pulse of high-tension current in the secondary windings of the coil. Burnt points may be caused only by age or neglect; but they may also be caused by an inefficient ignition condenser. The method of cleaning and, if necessary, renewing these points is described later in this chapter.

The Ignition Coil. The coil is the one item in the system which usually requires little attention. Beyond keeping the exterior surface clean and occasionally checking the tightness of the two low-tension terminals, there is little that can be done. The central high-tension terminal should be checked to ensure that it is clamped in the moulded cap of the coil. If any of the wires appears perished it should be renewed; frayed or corroded wiring at the terminals should be cut back and the connexions remade with sound wire. This applies also to any of the high-tension wires between the distributor and the sparking plugs.

THE DISTRIBUTOR

The distributor is mounted on top of the engine and is driven from the camshaft by the oil pump drive gear.

The Anglia 105E and Prefect 107E may have Lucas distributors (with the high-tension leads entering the side of the cap), or Autolite distributors (with vertically-mounted leads). Side-value engines have the earlier Lucas distributor shown in Fig. 25.

When the two spring clips on either side of the distributor have been released, the cap, complete with ignition cables, may be lifted off, revealing the rotor arm, contact-breaker mechanism and the condenser. As has already been described, the contact-breaker points interrupt the flow of low-tension current from the battery, through the ignition coil to "earth." Carefully wipe the inside and outside of the cap, paying particular attention to the spaces between the leads and terminals. Check that the small carbon brush in the centre of the cap of a Lucas distributor works freely in its holder, but be careful not to break it.

The contact point operated by the cam should be moved away from the fixed point with a finger to allow the two points to be examined. They should have a clean, grey frosted appearance. The formation of a slight "pip" on one point and a corresponding crater on the other is quite normal after several thousand miles of running. If the points are oily, they should be cleaned with a rag moistened with petrol. The contact-breaker lever carrying the movable point should be removed to allow the points to be cleaned or trued-up. This can be done by slackening the clamping nut on the low-tension terminal post and lifting the lever and spring off the pivot pin. The plate carrying the fixed point can then be removed.

Badly pitted or burnt contact points should be renewed; no amount of truing-up will make them serviceable. As replacement contacts must be fitted only as a pair it is necessary to remove the fixed contact by taking out the two locking screws. A careful note should be made of the position of any washers, particularly the insulating ones, for correct reassembly.

A single-unit contact-breaker assembly is used on late-type distributors, and this is, of course, a much easier proposition to remove and refit than the type shown at 3, 4 and 5 in Fig. 25.

It is a sound plan to fit new contact-breaker points and also a new condenser, whenever a new set of plugs is installed at 10,000-mile (16,000-km) intervals. The extra cost will be well repaid by improved performance, better petrol consumption and easier starting.

When reassembling the distributor a thin smear of petroleum jelly should be applied to the cam and a small drop of oil placed on the pivot pin before the movable contact point is fitted. At this stage the cam bearing and distributor shaft should be lightly lubricated. The distributor rotor should be pulled or gently prised off the cam spindle and a few drops of engine oil should be introduced through the aperture in the base plate through which the cam spindle passes. Test the freedom of the advance and retard weights by replacing the rotor and attempting to turn it in either direction by hand. It should turn slightly in one direction and spring back to the static position.

Contact-breaker Advance Mechanism. It should seldom be necessary to dismantle the distributor further than is necessary when renewing the contact points. If, however, the action of the advance-and-retard weights within the distributor body does not appear to be satisfactory—that is, if on rotating the distributor rotor in the direction of the arrow on the brass electrode the rotor does not spring back to its original position—the contact-breaker baseplate may be removed by extracting the two screws that pass through the projections on the edge of the baseplate and engage with the distributor body.

The two half-moon centrifugal weights will then be seen. If these appear to be binding or are rusty, they should be treated liberally with penetrating oil and moved outwards by hand against the tension of the retaining springs. It is a good plan, while the distributor is dismantled, to fit a new pair of springs. These cost very little and considerably influence the shape of the ignition advance curve, with a pronounced effect on the performance of the engine.

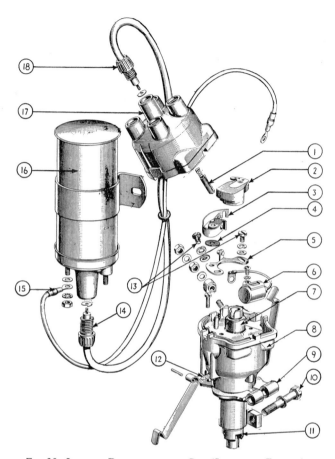

FIG. 25. IGNITION DISTRIBUTOR AND COIL (SIDE-VALVE ENGINES)

1. Distributor brush
2. Rotor
3. Contact-breaker moving arm
4. Insulating washer
5. Adjustable plate
6. Condenser
7. Cam
8. Distributor body
9. Split clamp
10. Bolt for clamp
11. Driving coupling
12. Timing scale
13. Contact plate screws
14. H.T. connector to coil
15. Connexion to C.B. terminal on coil
16. Coil
17. Distributor cap
18. H.T. connector to distributor cap

For example, if the springs have weakened they will allow too great a degree of ignition advance at low engine speeds and will cause excessive pinking. It is a simple matter to withdraw the weights and springs by unscrewing the retaining screw from the centre of the cam and drawing the cam upwards. First note the direction in which the slot in the cam, that engages with the rotor, is pointing so that the cam can be replaced in the same position.

Dismantling and reassembly just described is quite straightforward, the only point being that care must be taken not to overstretch the springs when refitting them. All parts should be liberally lubricated, preferably with a graphited oil.

Adjusting the Contact-breaker Gap. The contact-breaker points should be set when the fibre arm of the moving contact is on the highest point of the cam. Check the gap by sliding the feeler gauge squarely between the points. If a pip and crater have formed, it will be impossible to obtain a true reading. The points should, therefore, be renewed or re-faced as just described. There should be just a slight drag. If the gap is too small or too wide, adjustment is necessary; this is done by slackening the adjustment lock screws on the fixed contact plate and moving the plate.

For earlier engines the gap should be 15 thousandths of an inch (0·015 in., 0·397 mm). Later engines have Autolite distributors, for which the correct gap is 25 thousandths of an inch (0·0025 in., 0·635 mm).

After setting the gap, tighten the lock screws and make another check as it is possible slightly to alter the gap while tightening up the screws.

On later distributors, it will be seen that one end of the fixed contact plate is notched. This allows the tip of a screwdriver to be inserted and twisted to increase or decrease the gap between the points (see Fig. 26).

Timing the Ignition. If the ignition timing has been disturbed and a note has not been made of the original setting, the ignition must be retimed. Turn the engine until the notch on the crankshaft pulley lines up with the mark on the cylinder front cover with No. 1 piston at the top of its compression stroke. This can be ascertained by removing the other three sparking plugs and turning the engine by the fan belt or by the starting handle (when provided) until the compression of No. 1 piston is felt. Bring the notch on the pully slowly into line with the indicator on the timing cover.

On later engines there are two pointers embossed on the timing cover. The one nearest the centre of the engine gives an initial advance of 10°; the other an advance of 6°. If your engine requires 8°, set the notch on the pulley midway between the two pointers.

The distributor driving shaft in the cylinder head has two tongues which engage in corresponding slots in the distributor drive. These parts are machined off-centre to ensure correct engagement.

In the case of side-valve engines remove the distributor cap and fit the distributor on the engine with the index scale on the clamp plate between Nos. 2 and 3 sparking plugs. The rotor should now point towards No. 1 cylinder contact in the distributor cap. Fit the clamp screw and washer through the slot in the index scale and tighten down.

FIG. 26. CHECKING CONTACT-BREAKER GAP ON DISTRIBUTOR
FITTED TO OVERHEAD-VALVE ENGINES

A. Notch for screwdriver   D. Fixed contact
B. Rocking arm   E. Locking screw
C. Feeler gauge

Slacken the body clamp bolt and turn the distributor body clockwise until the points just begin to open, at the same time turning the rotor clockwise to take up any play in the drive.

On overhead-valve engines, having set the notch on the rim of the crankshaft pulley in line with the pointer on the timing chain cover with No. 1 piston at top-dead-centre on the compression stroke as just described, hold the distributor body so that the vacuum control unit spindle (when provided) is parallel with the engine and turn the rotor until its metal contact is in line with the low tension terminal as shown in Fig. 28. Now slide the distributor into place, noting that the rotor arm rotates towards the condenser as the helical gears engage.

Fit the screw and locking washer that secure the distributor clamp to the engine cylinder block. Check that the knurled timing adjustment nut is set so that the fourth line on the graduated scale is showing, and rotate the distributor in a clockwise direction to take up any backlash in the drive until the contact-breaker points are just about to open. Lock the distributor in this position by tightening the clamping bolt and nut.

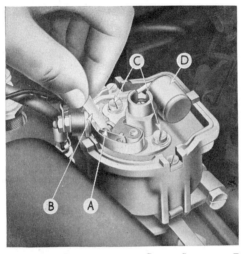

Fig. 27. Checking Contact-breaker Gap on Side-valve Engines

A. Moving contact point   C. Contact-plate locking screws
B. Feeler gauge   D. Condenser

Checking the Ignition Timing. In order to check the precise moment at which the points break contact a 6-watt bulb mounted in a suitable holder may be connected across the two low-tension terminals at the top of the ignition coil. The ignition should be switched on and the engine rotated. When the points are closed the lamp will light up; at the instant they open it will be extinguished. It is a simple matter, therefore, to set the engine to top-dead centre as just described, slacken the distributor clamp, turn the distributor anti-clockwise until the lamp lights up, and then clockwise until it is just extinguished.

It will be noticed that it is recommended that with overhead-valve engines the distributor index scale should be set with the zero mark against the index mark or with four divisions showing on later distributors. When premium fuel is used, however, the scale may be advanced by one or two divisions but the ignition should not be advanced to such an extent that the engine becomes rough and refuses to pull well at low speeds.

The setting can be checked with a standard grade petrol, as described at the beginning of Chapter 2, to give light pinking at low speeds on full throttle uphill the pinking should disappear by the time a speed of 30 m.p.h. (50 k.p.h.) is reached.

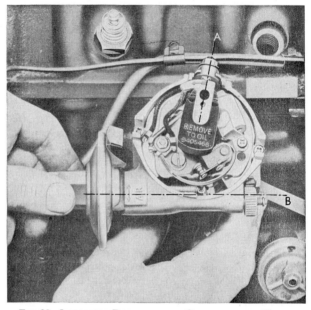

FIG. 28. INSTALLING DISTRIBUTOR ON OVERHEAD-VALVE ENGINE
A. Rotor in line with terminal   *B.* Vacuum control parallel to cylinder block

This method of setting the ignition is a little crude by modern standards, however, and cannot be employed when premium petrol is used, since under ordinary conditions the engine will not pink on this fuel, even when over-advanced. An excessive amount of ignition advance can be detrimental to the engine.

The most effective method of setting the timing when premium fuels are used is to make a series of tests on a level road, noting carefully, by stopwatch readings, the time taken to accelerate from 20 m.p.h. to 50 m.p.h. in top gear with the throttle fully open in each case and over the same stretch of road, so that each test is conducted under precisely similar conditions. The best ignition setting is that which results in the shortest time to accelerate over this speed range. This will also give the most economical fuel consumption.

If a stop-watch is not available an alternative scheme is to start each test from a given point and to note carefully the point at which the higher speed is reached, by reference to bushes by the roadside, fencing posts or similar identifying marks. It must be remembered that only slight movements of the distributor will be required, since one division on the scale

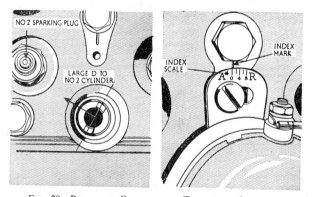

FIG. 29. POINTS TO CHECK WHEN TIMING THE IGNITION ON SIDE-VALVE ENGINES

The distributor driving coupling must be in the position shown and the distributor clamp should be tightened when the zero mark on the scale is opposite the index mark (as described in the text)

is equivalent to four degrees of ignition advance or retard on the engine flywheel. Remember too, that if the contact-breaker points are readjusted, opening the points slightly will advance the ignition while closing the gap will retard it.

THE SPARKING PLUGS

Difficult starting or misfiring can be caused by dirty sparking plugs or incorrect plug gaps. It is important, therefore, that both the inside and outside of the sparking plugs should receive regular attention. The portion of the insulator projecting above the body of the sparking plug should be kept clean by wiping it with a dry, clean rag. *The only effective method of cleaning the interior insulator and the inside of the plug is to use a garage plug-cleaning and testing machine.*

When the car is left standing with the engine cold and the atmosphere is damp, it is possible for moisture to condense on the external surface of the insulator, although the anti-condensation caps that are fitted as standard will usually prevent this trouble. If a wet path exists from the plug terminal to the plug body, however, through which the high-tension current can pass to earth instead of jumping the gap at the plug points, difficult starting can be expected.

DIAGNOSING SPARKING-PLUG TROUBLES

PLUG CONDITION	POSSIBLE CAUSE	REMEDY
Insulator and body—clean, coloured straw to coffee	Plug in correct condition	
Insulator and body—fluffy grey deposit	Plug in correct condition Deposit due to premium petrol	Clean plug and reset gap
Gap—too wide or too narrow	Incorrect adjustment	Set gap to manufacturer's recommendation
Insulator—clean, coloured straw to coffee Body—hard carbon deposits	Too much oil Unsuitable oil Too much upper cylinder lubricant	Check piston rings Check level of oil in sump Reduce upper-cylinder lubricant
Insolator—clean, white or pale Electrodes—partly worn (after short service) Body—clean	Plug too *hot* Mixture too lean Ignition too far advanced	Fit *cooler* plug Adjust carburettor for richer mixture Retard spark
Insulator—sooted up Body—sooty	Mixture too rich Ignition too far retarded Plug too *cool*	Check for excessive use of choke Adjust carburettor for leaner mixture Advance spark Fit *hotter* plug
Insulator and body—sooted and oiled up	Plug too *cool* Too much oil Mixture too rich	Fit *hotter* plug Check piston rings Check level of oil in sump Reduce upper-cylinder lubricant Adjust carburettor for leaner mixture
Insulator—cracked inside Body—clean	Damaged during electrode adjustment Plug too *hot* Mixture too lean	Fit new plug, adjust gap by bending side electrode *only* Fit *cooler* plug Adjust carburettor for richer mixture
Insulator—dark, blistered, cracked or partly glazed Electrodes—badly worn, eaten away Body—clean or covered with grey deposit	Plug too *hot* for premium petrol	Fit *cooler* plug for use with premium petrol

The same trouble can occur when dust accumulates on an oily insulator, providing a "track" to earth. If difficulty is experienced in starting, therefore, particularly in winter months, do not continue to operate the starter as further troubles could arise from its prolonged use; first wipe the sparking plug insulators, caps and rubber leads. Unless other ignition faults are present the engine should then start readily.

Prolonged use of the starter causes conditions to become worse instead of better. First, the sparking plug internal insulators become wet with petrol, preventing a spark occurring at the plug points. This will necessitate the removal of the plugs and warming them to dry the internal insulators—an operation which may have to be carried out more than once because of the large amount of petrol present in the combustion

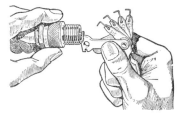

FIG. 30. ADJUSTING SPARKING PLUG GAP

chambers. Secondly if the battery is in a low state of charge the voltage will be further reduced and may be insufficient for the ignition circuit during the period when the starting motor is operating.

Adjusting Sparking Plug Gaps. Throughout its working life the plug is subjected to very high temperatures. Inevitably, after some thousands of miles of use, the gap between the electrodes will have widened. It should, therefore, be checked and adjusted at regular intervals. Check the gap with the sparking plug gauge and make any adjustment that may be necessary by bending the side electrode. Most gap-setting tools are specially shaped for this purpose. Otherwise, the side electrode may be tapped towards the central one either on the bench or with a suitable tool. If the gap is closed too much, do not use the central electrode as a support when levering the side electrode up; this may crack the insulator.

The feeler blade—or, better still, a wire-type plug gauge (Fig. 30)—should just slide between the electrodes when the gap is set at 0·025 in., (0·635 mm) which is the correct figure for all types of plugs. In the absence of a gauge of this thickness a normal combination-set of mechanic's feelers should be used, the required thickness being made by using two or more blades together.

The threaded portion of the plugs should be cleaned with a stiff wire brush and a smear of graphite-grease placed on the threads. This will ensure that the plugs will tighten down easily and facilitate removal when the next cleaning and adjustment is due. Make sure that the copper-asbestos washers are in good condition and tighten the plugs, using hand pressure only on the tommy bar to ensure a gas-tight joint. Too much force should never be used and is unnecessary.

Sparking Plugs as a Guide to Engine Condition. Irregularities in carburation, distribution, and so on can usually be detected by examining the internal insulators of the sparking plugs *see* the chart on page 62. It is essential that the engine should be switched off while it is running at a reasonably high speed. This avoids the clouding effect produced by the idling mixture (which is richer than the normal mixture).

Plugs that run hotter or cooler than the standard grades recommended in Chapter 8 are listed in the plug manufacturers' charts or booklets that can be seen at most garages and accessory shops.

5 Electrical system and auxiliaries

A generator of the two-brush compensated-voltage-control type is fitted. The charging rate is automatically controlled by a regulator unit, housed with the cut-out in the control box, and will depend entirely on the state of charge of the battery—it is not under the control of the driver.

The regulator automatically provides a large charging current when the battery is discharged, so that the battery is brought back to a fully-charged state in the shortest possible time; on the other hand, a low "trickle" charge is provided for a fully-charged battery, in order to keep it in good condition without the possibility of damage or excessive "gassing" due to overcharging.

The cut-out is a form of automatic switch which connects and disconnects the battery from the dynamo whenever the engine is stopped or is running at low speeds.

Ammeter or Charge Indicator. The ammeter is connected into the main lead between the battery and the electrical circuits with the exception of the starter and horn circuits. The charge indicator or generator warning light merely indicates that current is flowing in the circuit and that the battery is being charged or discharged; it does not give any indication of the state of charge of the battery, except that when a two-brush voltage-controlled generator is fitted the ammeter will show a relatively high charging rate when the battery charge is low and a low charging rate when the battery is nearly fully charged. The indicator should never show a constant high discharge reading when the engine is running at normal speeds; if it does so, the generator and regulator should be tested.

Dynamo Maintenance and Testing. If charging is not satisfactory (indicated by the state of the battery) first ascertain that the dynamo belt tension is correct (see Chapter 1).

A low charging rate can often be traced to a dirty or pitted dynamo commutator, or to chipped, worn or binding carbon brushes. On early models a cover band can be removed from the end of the dynamo to allow the commutator and brushes to be inspected. Carefully raise the brush springs with a hooked wire and extract the brushes. Clean out the brush holders with a cloth dipped in petrol. Next clean the commutator by pressing a petrol-damped cloth against it while rotating it by the pulley, after slackening the belt drive. If the commutator is slightly burnt, it can be burnished by using a strip of fine glass-paper folded around a flat piece of wood. Press the glass-paper on the commutator while the engine is idling. Emery cloth should never be used to clean the commutator. If the commutator is badly pitted or scored the dynamo should be returned to the agents for attention.

When replacing the brushes make sure that they are free to move in their holders and bed down properly on the commutator; also check that the brush springs have not lost their tension. The spring tension should not be increased unnecessarily, however, as this will simply lead to rapid wear of the brushes.

If the brushes are found to be tight or sticking after the holders have been cleaned, their width may be slightly reduced by rubbing them down on a sheet of glass-paper laid on a flat surface such as a sheet of plate-glass.

If the brushes are badly worn or cracked, remove the screws securing the eyelets on the ends of the brush leads. Fit the new brushes into their holders and secure the eyelets on the end of the brush leads in the original positions. New brushes are preformed to the commutator surface and do not require further bedding down.

On later cars a removable cover is not fitted but the commutator can be inspected through the ventilation aperture in the end-plate of the generator. If the commutator or brushes need attention it will be necessary to dismantle the dynamo; this is normally a job that is best entrusted to your authorized dealer.

If a moving-coil voltmeter, reading from 0 to 20 volts, is available it may be used to test the dynamo when the engine is running. The two leads at the rear of the dynamo should be disconnected and the two terminals bridged with a short length of copper wire. One of the voltmeter leads should then be connected to the dynamo terminals and the other to a good earthing point on the dynamo frame. Note the voltmeter readings as the engine speed is gradually increased. A reading of 12 volts should be obtained at a fast idling speed (the engine should not be run at a higher speed with the dynamo disconnected). If no reading is obtained throughout the test, first check the voltmeter connexions; if there is no improvement the dynamo should be removed for examination.

DYNAMO AND CHARGING SYSTEM FAULTS

As a quick check on whether the battery is well charged and the cables and connections are in good condition, switch on the headlights and operate the starter. If the lights dim only slightly and the starter turns the engine at normal speed, it can be assumed that the battery and main wiring system are sound.

If the lights become very dim or go out when the starter is operated, check first for loose or dirty connections at the battery terminals, at the starter motor or solenoid operated-switch and at the connection between the battery earthing cable and the bodywork. A rusty or corroded contact here is often overlooked. If these checks are satifactory, have the battery tested by a service station which possesses the correct equipment.

These preliminary checks should always be made before attempting to diagnose any of the faults listed below.

Symptom	*Probable Cause*
Battery Charge **Consistently Low** A low state of charge may be due simply to the drain caused by frequent starting, short journeys and night driving, when the output from the dynamo is often insufficient to meet the current drawn from the battery. During the winter months it may be necessary to use a trickle charger regularly in such circumstances. But first check for the faults in the next column.	Defective battery. Sulphated plates will not accept a full charge. Buckled plates or an accumulation of sediment will cause internal leakage of current. Have battery checked by an expert. Loose dynamo driving belt. Check tension of belt and adjust if necessary. Insufficient output from dynamo. Have output tested by service station. New brushes may be required or a replacement dynamo may be needed. Faulty dynamo regulator. A moving-coil voltmeter is needed when checking and adjusting the regulator. Again a job for the expert. Loose connections or a broken wire in charging circuit.
Battery Consistently **Overcharged** This fault is indicated by the need for frequent topping-up of the battery with distilled water.	Regulator set to give too high a charging rate. Have setting checked by a service station.

Control Box. The cut-out and regulator are carefully set before they leave the manufacturer's works and should not be tampered with. If, however, the dynamo output does not fall when the battery is fully charged, or the battery becomes abnormally discharged, it will be necessary to call in expert assistance.

The owner should never attempt to carry out adjustments as the use of an accurately calibrated moving-coil voltmeter is essential in order to obtain the correct settings.

The cut-out can also be checked. The points should close as soon as the engine is speeded up slightly above the normal idling speed.

The regulator and cut-out contacts may be cleaned by inserting a strip of fine glass-paper between them, closing the contacts with a finger and drawing the glass-paper through several times with the rough side toward each contact point in turn.

BATTERY

The battery is of the 12-volt lead-acid type with seven plates per cell. The battery compartment is on the right-hand side of the engine compartment. For this reason fairly frequent inspection is required because of the tendency for the engine heat to evaporate the distilled water. The frequency of topping-up can be reduced by arranging some form of shield to deflect the fan blast from the battery.

The vent plugs should be kept clean and tight to prevent acid leakage and the battery and the surrounding parts, particularly the tops of the cells, clean and dry. If acid is spilled, wipe it away with a clean wet cloth and then dry the part thoroughly; household ammonia will neutralize the acid. The terminals and connexions should be kept free from corrosion and should be smeared with a coating of petroleum jelly.

The level of the electrolyte in the cells of the battery should not be allowed to fall below the tops of the separators; a check should be made at least once a week to ensure that the level is $\frac{1}{4}$ in. to $\frac{3}{8}$ in. (6 to 9 mm) above the separators. Distilled water only should be added until this level is reached in each cell. It is best to add water just before the cells are to be charged. In cold weather this will allow the acid and water to mix thoroughly and thus avoid any risk of the water freezing and damaging the plates and battery case. It should not be necessary to add acid unless some of the electrolyte has been spilt. If acid is added in order to raise the specific gravity of the electrolyte, the plates may be damaged.

The need for excessive topping-up of all cells is usually an indication of an unduly high generator charging rate, while if one cell regularly requires more water than the others, a leak in that cell must be suspected. Even a slow leak may, in time, completely drain the acid from a cell. A leaky container should, of course, be replaced immediately, and all parts that have been exposed to the acid should be well swabbed with household ammonia to prevent corrosion.

Specific Gravity of the Electrolyte. The best indication of the state of charge of the cells is the specific gravity of the electrolyte, which can be ascertained by using a hydrometer. The readings for each of the cells should be approximately the same. A reading should not be taken immediately after adding distilled water, however; the battery should be charged for at least an hour to ensure that the water and acid are thoroughly mixed.

A battery in a low state of charge may be recharged by making a long run in daylight or by charging from a d.c. supply at a rate of 5 amp until the cells are "gassing" freely.

The electrolyte drawn into the hydrometer should be fairly clear; if it is dirty it is probable that the plates are in a bad condition, in which case the Ford service or battery agent should be consulted.

The specific gravity of the acid in the cells when fully charged should be within 0·005 (5 points) above or 0·010 (10 points) below the values given in the tables below—

TEMPERATE CLIMATES

Air temperature ordinarily below 90°F (32°C)

CONDITION OF CELL	ACTUAL HYDROMETER READING AT TEMPERATURE OF						
	50°F (10°C)	60°F (16°C)	70°F (21°C)	80°F (27°C)	90°F (32°C)	100°F (38°C)	110°F (43°C)
Fully charged .	1·288	1·284	1·280	1·276	1·272	1·268	1·264
Half charged .	1·208	1·204	1·200	1·197	1·193	1·189	1·186
Fully discharged	1·116	1·113	1·110	1·108	1·104	1·101	1·098

TROPICAL AND SUB-TROPICAL CLIMATES

(Note that the capacity of the battery is somewhat reduced since an acid of lower specific gravity is used)

CONDITION OF CELL	ACTUAL HYDROMETER READING AT TEMPERATURE OF						
	60°F (16°C)	70°F (21°C)	80°F (27°C)	90°F (32°C)	100°F (38°C)	110°F (43°C)	125°F (52°C)
Fully charged .	1·214	1·210	1·206	1·202	1·198	1·195	1·190
Half charged .	1·163	1·160	1·156	1·153	1·150	1·147	1·141
Fully discharged	1·102	1·100	1·097	1·093	1·090	1·087	1·083

Specific Gravity Too Low. If the specific gravity after a prolonged charge is persistently less than the "fully charged" values, it is possible that it may be necessary to add acid to bring the specific gravity up to the correct figure. Whenever possible, however, expert advice should be sought on this point.

Low Specific Gravity in One Cell. This fault (especially if successive readings show the difference to be increasing), indicates that the cell is in poor condition. If the specific gravity is 0·050 to 0·075 below that in the other cells and there is no leakage of electrolyte, a partial short-circuit or

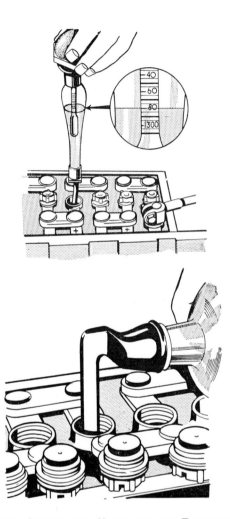

FIG. 31. TESTING BATTERY WITH HYDROMETER AND TOPPING-UP CELLS

70

other trouble within the cell is indicated and the local Ford dealer should be consulted.

Idle Batteries. A battery which is to stand idle should be charged at the normal charging rate until the specific gravity is within 0·010 of the fully-charged value. Disconnect the wires from the battery to avoid loss of charge through any small leak in the wiring.

A battery not in active service may be kept in condition for immediate use by giving it a freshening charge at least once every two months. It should, preferably, also be given a thorough charge after an idle period before it is put into service. It is unwise to allow a battery that is in good condition to stand for more than two months without charging it.

Keeping the Battery Charged. The battery being the "reservoir" for the energy generated by the dynamo, once it is full there is no object in delivering further current to it. While it is always better to keep a battery overcharged rather than undercharged, it should be remembered that extremes of undercharging or overcharging will tend to shorten the life of the battery.

Obviously, the amount of charging required will depend on how you use the car. If the car is used for short runs in town, with consequent frequent use of the starter, the battery will naturally require more charging than when it is used for long-distance runs. Then again, the demands on the battery are generally greater in winter than in summer—the lamps are more frequently used and the starter takes more current when turning over a cold engine. In these circumstances it may be necessary to keep the battery in good condition by the overnight use of a trickle-charger.

STARTER MOTOR

When starting from cold pull out the "choke" control knob (the engine should never be run, when warmed up, with this control in action). In very cold weather it may be an advantage to depress the clutch pedal to eliminate the drag of the lubricant in the gearbox and prevent unnecessary strain on the starter motor and battery. On the other hand, the friction of the clutch release bearing may slow down the cranking speed. It is advisable to make a test under both conditions. Operate the starter switch firmly and release it immediately the engine fires.

If the starter is sluggish in action, it should be removed from the engine and the commutator and brushes cleaned, preferably by an expert. Assuming that the battery is in a charged condition, the starter should rotate the engine smartly when the switch is operated. The headlamps should be switched on during the test. If the lights go dim, although the starter does not operate, the indication is that the battery is discharged or that current is flowing through the windings of the starter but for some

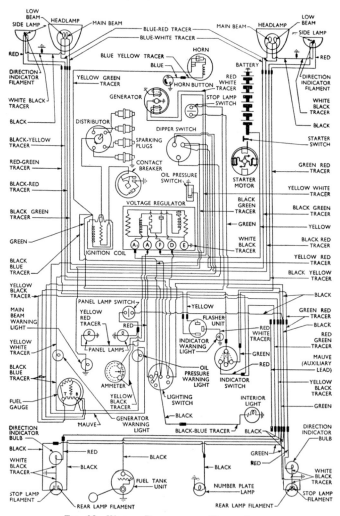

FIG. 32. WIRING DIAGRAM FOR EARLY ANGLIA

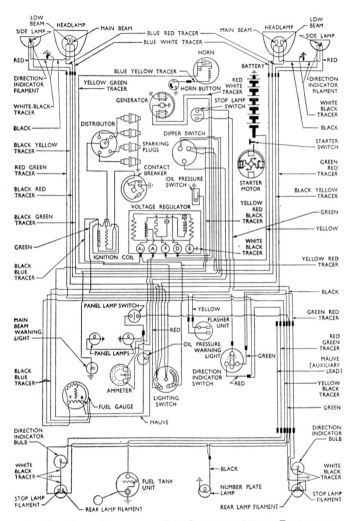

FIG. 33. Wiring Diagram for Late Side-valve Anglia, Escort and 5-cwt van. For overhead-valve vans, *see* Fig. 34

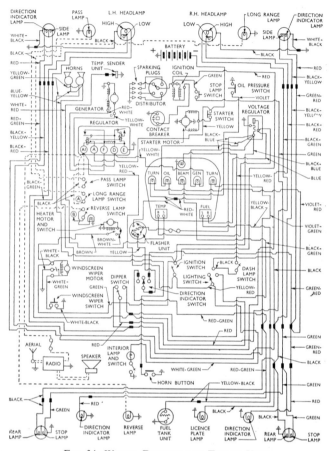

FIG. 34. WIRING DIAGRAM FOR THAMES VANS

The circuit shown is for de luxe vehicles. Since approximately September 1963, standard vehicles have not been provided with oil-pressure or main-beam warning lights. The fuel gauge is now of the "balancing coil" type, therefore no instrument voltage regulator is required. Dotted circuits are for accessories only. (*A*) When both pass and long-range lights are fitted, this feed may be connected to the pass-light switch to simplify wiring. (*B*) Connect to the rear-light circuit when a reverse light is fitted

74

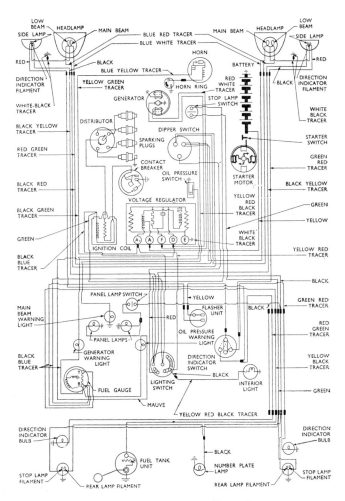

FIG. 35. WIRING DIAGRAM FOR EARLY PREFECT

reason the armature is not rotating, possibly owing to the starter pinion being already engaged with the flywheel starter-ring.

Should the lamps remain bright, however, the starter switch may be inoperative and should be checked.

The cable-operated type of switch used on earlier models can be tested by moving the switch lever by hand. If the starter then operates, the cable will probably be found to be loose at one attachment point, stretched or binding. If there is no response from the starter when the switch arm is pulled firmly, the cleanness and tightness of the terminals on the switch should be checked. A possible trouble is burnt contacts within the switch, which must then be renewed as a complete assembly.

On later cars which have a solenoid (electro-magnetic) starter switch that is controlled by the ignition-switch, the trouble must either be caused by a faulty solenoid (which is not repairable) or by a break or a poor contact in the wiring between the ignition switch and the solenoid, or between the solenoid and the starter motor or battery.

Freeing a Jammed Starter Pinion. If the starter pinion should become jammed in mesh with the starter ring it can usually be freed by engaging top gear and attempting to rock the car forward. Do not engage a lower gear and rock the car backwards and forwards; this may jam the pinion more firmly in mesh and may damage the drive. If it is difficult to free the pinion, the small dust cap should be prised off the end of the starter and the squared end of the shaft turned in a clockwise direction with a spanner.

If the starter pinion does not engage with the flywheel, the starter drive probably requires cleaning. It will be necessary to unbolt the starter from the engine. The pinion should move freely on the screwed sleeve; if there is any dirt on the sleeve it must be washed off with paraffin. A trace of light machine oil should then be applied to the sleeve; engine oil must not be used owing to the risk of grit accumulating on the sleeve and causing the pinion to stick. If the battery is discharged or weak, the starter may spin once or twice without engaging—this is a useful pointer to a source of trouble that may result in one being stranded until a new battery or a tow can be obtained.

AUXILIARIES AND INSTRUMENTS

Aligning the Headlamps. The headlamps should be aligned with the car empty, standing on a level surface 25 ft (7·6 m) away from a white wall or screen, which should be in semi-darkness or sufficiently shielded from direct light so that the light spots from the headlamps can be seen clearly. The aligning points shown in Fig. 41 should be marked on it. Remove the headlamp masks by undoing the screws at top and bottom. The beams can then be aligned by screwing the vertical or horizontal adjustment screws inwards or outwards.

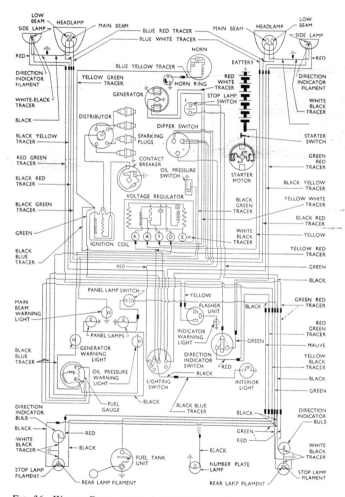

FIG. 36. WIRING DIAGRAM FOR LATE SIDE-VALVE PREFECT AND SQUIRE

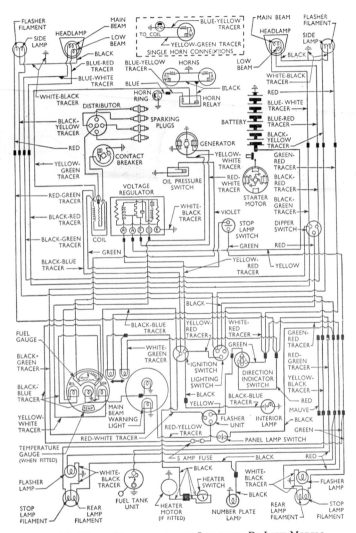

FIG. 37. WIRING DIAGRAM FOR ALL SIDE-VALVE DE LUXE MODELS

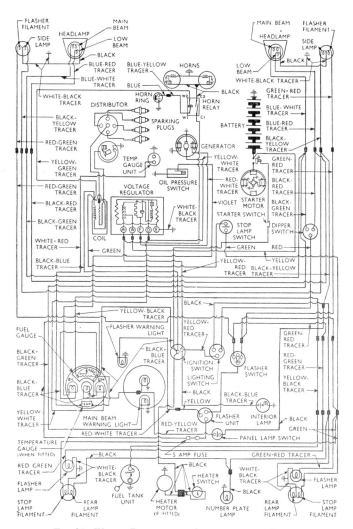

Fig. 38. Wiring Diagram for Overhead-valve Prefect

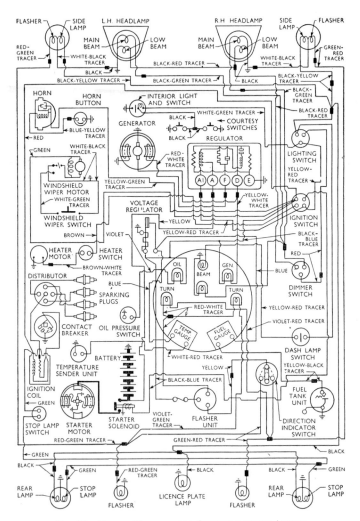

FIG. 39. WIRING DIAGRAM FOR OVERHEAD-VALVE ANGLIA

The Anglia Super is very similar, apart from the provision of a cigarette lighter

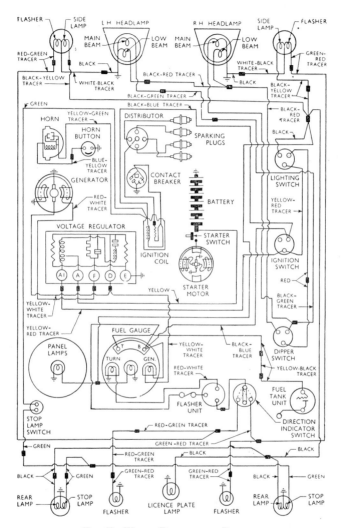

FIG. 40. WIRING DIAGRAM FOR POPULAR

Fuel Gauge. On all models except those from late 1962 onwards, the fuel gauge contains two small electro-magnets which control the gauge needle. If the gauge does not give the correct readings first make sure that current is reaching the *B* terminal on the dashboard instrument when the ignition is switched on. If this is the case, disconnect the lead from the *T* terminal. The pointer should now remain against the FULL mark. Now reconnect the lead to the gauge and earth it at the tank unit end. The gauge should then read EMPTY. From this it can be deduced that, if the pointer normally remains at FULL, there is probably a break in the circuit between the gauge and the tank unit. If it remains at EMPTY, the wire running to the tank unit may be short-circuited at some point. In either case, however, the possibility of a faulty instrument or tank unit cannot be ruled out and it would be as well to ask a Ford dealer to make a test by substituting replacement units.

In the case of the more recent type of gauge, the pointer (which takes several seconds to register the correct reading after the ignition has been switched on) is deflected by a bi-metal strip which bends as current passes through a heating coil wound around it. A small voltage regulator supplies current at 10 volts to the gauge. The tank instrument is similar to that used with the electro-magnetic type of gauge.

Fault-tracing with this type of gauge is confined to making sure that current is reaching the voltage regulator and that this is supplying the correct voltage. If necessary, fit a replacement regulator, making sure that the *B* and *E* terminals are uppermost and are not more than 20 degrees from the vertical. If the gauge still does not operate correctly when the ignition is switched on, there is little that can be done except to check for the continuity of the wiring between the gauge and the tank unit and then to substitute a serviceable unit for each in turn.

Speedometer. The speedometer head requires comparatively little servicing and, as special equipment is required for most repair work, it is advisable to send the head to the makers or authorized speedometer service station for overhaul.

If the speedometer cable becomes noisy in operation, however, or the speedometer needle wavers or jerks, the trouble will usually be that the driving cable requires lubrication, preferably with a graphited grease.

The cable should be disconnected at the head and pulled out from the upper end of the conduit. If the old cable is broken it may be necessary to remove the lower piece from the transmission end of the conduit by unscrewing the connexion at the lower end.

After lubricating the cable, slide it back into the conduit. The lower end can be engaged with the driving spindle on the gearbox shaft by rotating the cable with the fingers and pressing it gently but firmly downwards until the cable is felt to engage. The upper end should then engage with the speedometer driving spindle without difficulty. Do not fully tighten the

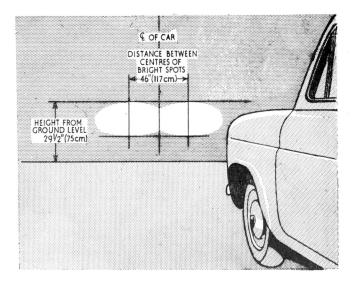

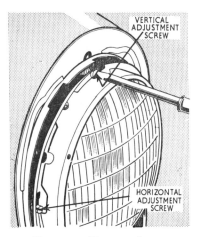

Fig. 41. Aligning Headlamps (Showing Spring-loaded Adjusting Screws)

retaining sleeve until the car has been driven a few yards to ensure that the connexions at each end are fully "home."

Windscreen Wiper. On the earlier Anglia and on the Prefect and Popular the wiper is vacuum-operated and is brought into use by turning the control knob to the right while the engine is running. Partial movement of the control will reduce the speed of operation.

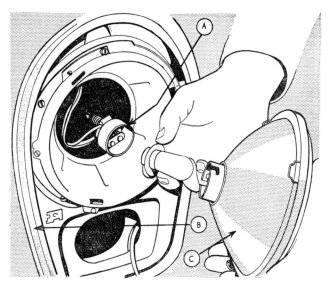

FIG. 42. RENEWING HEADLAMP BULB

The bulb socket (A) has been removed from the reflector (C). The rubber sealing strip (B) must be maintained in good condition. Later cars have sealed-beam units instead of separate bulbs, reflectors, and lamp glasses

The power to operate the wiper is obtained from the pressure of the atmosphere, which acts first on one side and then on the other of a pivoted paddle blade, swinging from side to side in an airtight casing. The air on the opposite side of the paddle blade, on each stroke, is drawn out by the partial vacuum existing in the induction system of the engine.

It will be evident that the most likely source of trouble is in the rubber tubing connecting the various units. If the tubing is perished or split it should be renewed. If the motor itself is defective, however, this is definitely a job that is best left to a Ford service station owing to the fact that special tools are desirable to service the motor properly. The best plan is to take advantage of the service by which you can obtain a reconditioned wiper in exchange for your faulty unit.

On Anglia models from September 1959 onwards an electrically-operated windscreen wiper is fitted. The motor is brought into action by pulling out the control knob on the dashboard. The wiper blades will park automatically when the knob is pushed home to switch off the motor. The wiper motor and gearbox are lubricated during assembly and require no attention over a very long period. If the wiper becomes defective and it is established that the switch or the wiring are not at fault, it is as well to call in the services of a Ford dealer.

6 The hydraulic brakes and clutch

THE braking system on all models is hydraulically-operated. The hand-brake operates on the rear wheels only, through a cable linkage, whereas the footbrake pedal operates the brakes on all four wheels.

The hydraulic system (Figs. 43, 45, 46 and 47) comprises a master cylinder in which the hydraulic pressure is originated, a cylinder or cylinders operating the brake shoes in each brake drum, a reservoir from which the brake fluid in the system is replenished, and the pipelines connecting the master cylinder to the wheel cylinders.

When the brake pedal is operated the master cylinder piston applies a force to the fluid which, being virtually incompressible, causes the wheel cylinder pistons to expand the brake shoes until they touch the brake drums. This limits the amount of pedal travel and further effort on the pedal increases the force applied to the brake shoes. The pressure generated in the master cylinder is transmitted equally and without loss to the pistons of each wheel cylinder so that the forces applied to the various shoes are identical and balanced braking is obtained.

When the pressure on the foot pedal is released the brake shoe pull-off springs force the wheel cylinder pistons back and the fluid passes back to the master cylinder, ready for the next application of the brakes.

Routine Maintenance. One of the main features of hydraulic brakes is that routine attention is reduced to a minimum, being confined primarily to checking, at 5,000-mile intervals, the fluid level in the supply tank, which should be topped up to within $\frac{1}{4}$ in. (6·35 mm) below the base of the reservoir filler neck with genuine EnFo brake fluid. The supply tank should not be filled completely.

Insufficient fluid in the reservoir can result in air entering the brake operating system, causing a "spongy" feel when the brake pedal is depressed.

Topping-up should be necessary only at long intervals. A rapid or considerable fall in the fluid level indicates either overfilling or a leak at some point in the system, which should be traced and rectified.

To check for leaks have an assistant pump the brake pedal once or twice and then hold it down firmly while you examine each pipeline connexion.

Alternatively a periodic check of the hydraulic system can be carried out by adjusting the brake shoes until they are hard on the drums. The brake pedal should then be pumped hard once or twice and heavy pressure

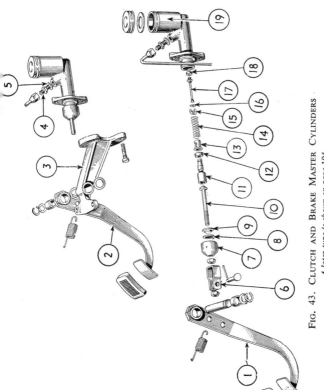

FIG. 43. CLUTCH AND BRAKE MASTER CYLINDERS

A later type is shown on page 104

1. Brake pedal
2. Clutch pedal
3. Supporting bracket
4. Union adaptor
5. Washer
6. Clevis or yoke
7. Dust-excluding cover

8. Circlip
9. Piston retaining washer
10. Push rod
11. Piston
12. Piston seal
13. Spring retainer
14. Piston return spring

15. Spacer
16. Valve seal
17. Valve stem
18. Valve seal
19. Fluid reservoir

maintained for a minute or two. If the pedal withstands this pressure it can be assumed, as a rough check, that the hydraulic system is in order and free from leaks.

BRAKING SYSTEM FAULTS

Excessive Pedal Travel	Brakes require adjustment (see Chapter 6). If fault occurs only after prolonged or excessive use of brakes, it is caused by "brake fade." Normal braking will be restored when brakes cool down.
Brake Pedal Feels Spongy or Requires Pumping to Operate Brakes	Air in hydraulic system. Check level of fluid in reservoir, top-up if necessary and bleed brakes (see Chapter 6). Check for leaks throughout.
	Main cup in master cylinder worn. Have components renewed by service station.
	Excessive end-float on front-wheel hub bearings.
Brakes Lack Power (*See also* "Excessive Pedal Travel," above)	Worn friction linings, or oil or grease on linings. Fit replacements (*see* Chapter 6).
	Scored or dirtorted brake drums. Fit new drums.
	Defective piston cups or seals in wheel or master cylinders. Have new parts fitted throughout.
	Defective brake servo (when fitted).
Brakes Bind	Handbrake adjustment too tight or cable binding.
	Swollen piston or seal in brake cylinder or master cylinder.
	Compensating port in master cylinder obstructed by grit or swollen main cup. Master cylinder should be overhauled by an expert.
	Defective brake servo (when fitted).
Brakes Grab	Friction linings or pads contaminated with oil or grease. Sometimes the brakes may grab slightly after the car has stood overnight in damp weather. This is not a serious fault, if symptom disappears during normal running.
	Loose front hub bearing.
	Distorted or badly scored drum.
Brakes Pull to One Side	Unequal tyre pressures.
	Grease or oil on friction linings.
	Worn or glazed friction linings.
	Restriction in flexible brake hose or faulty operating cylinder in brake on opposite side to which steering pulls.
	Wear in front suspension or steering components.

Brake Adjustment. When pedal travel becomes excessive the brake shoes must be adjusted to compensate for wear of the brake linings.

Before beginning work, first make sure that the tyres are inflated to the correct pressure and that the front wheel bearings have not excessive bearing "play."

Jack up the car to allow each wheel to be adjusted in turn, and ensure that the wheel rotates freely. The handbrake, of course, should be in the fully released position when adjusting the rear brakes, at least one wheel being securely chocked to prevent movement.

On earlier cars there are two hexagonal-headed adjusters on each front brake backplate and one on each rear brake backplate (*see* Fig. 44). On later cars, square-headed adjusters are fitted. In this case, the pre-set adjuster on the rear brakes (which should not be disturbed) may be mistaken for the normal service adjuster, which also has a square head. The latter can be identified by its projecting threaded shaft.

In each case the method of adjustment is the same. Spin the wheel and tighten up each adjuster by turning the hexagon nut clockwise until the wheels are locked on the drum, and then slacken back the adjuster one "click" at a time until the wheel rotates freely. This adjustment should

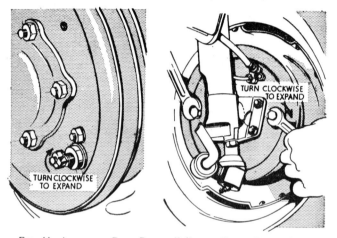

FIG. 44. ADJUSTING REAR BRAKE (*left*) AND FRONT BRAKE (*right*)

be done with the brake drums cold. Repeat this procedure with the other adjusters, but remember that there is only *one* square-headed adjuster on each rear brake.

The adjusters usually become very stiff and it is only too easy to burr-over the flats if an ordinary spanner is used. The best plan is to buy a special brake-adjusting spanner from an accessory shop, such as Halfords.

The brakes should now be tested on the road and a good stretch of dry surface, preferably uncambered, should be selected for the purpose. The brakes should be applied hard at about 30 m.p.h. and the braking marks should be examined to determine whether any wheel is locking before the remainder. It should also be noted whether there is a tendency to pull towards one side of the road.

If it is found that the brakes are inefficient or unbalanced, the cause is probably grease on the linings. It is extremely important that the linings should be kept free from grease and oil. The use of correct front wheel bearing lubricant and care not to overfill the back axle, as well as replacing grease retainers when leakage is indicated, will help to maintain braking efficiency. If the linings are badly saturated with grease or oil, new, relined brake shoes should be fitted.

A common cause of brakes squeaking, grabbing or losing efficiency is an accumulation of dust (most of which is worn off the friction linings) inside the drums. It is a wise precaution to take the drums off at 5,000-mile (8,000-km) intervals (as described below) so that the dust can be brushed or blown out and at the same time the condition of the friction lining can be checked. The linings should never be allowed to wear down until the rivets are flush with the working surfaces. Renew them when there is about $\frac{1}{16}$ in. (1·6 mm) of wear left.

Fitting Replacement Shoes. At some time during the life of the car it will be necessary to fit replacement brake shoes. This is best done by an authorized Ford agent, but if the following instructions are carried out the operations should not present any difficulties to the keen owner.

After jacking up the car and removing the road wheels, slacken off the brake adjuster fully and then remove the combined hub and drum, exposing the brake shoes. A hub extractor will probably be required for the rear hubs. Consult your Ford dealer.

Rest a large screwdriver against one of the bolts on the backplate and lever one shoe out of the groove in the end of the piston in the wheel cylinder. Do not over-stretch the shoe pull-off springs when removing the shoes.

Clean down the backplate and brake drum. Check the adjuster unit for ease of movement and lubricate it with special brake grease. Slacken back (anti-clockwise) the adjuster to the fully off position.

To fit replacement shoes, detach the springs from the old shoes and fit them to the new shoes. On the front brakes hook the spring of one shoe into the hole in the backplate, fit the shoe into the inclined abutment at the rear of one wheel cylinder and with the screwdriver under the web of the shoe, ease the shoe into the groove in the end of the hydraulic piston. Repeat with the second shoe.

With the back shoes the procedure is somewhat different. In this case, couple the shoes together by the two pull-off springs, remembering that the longer spring is nearer the wheel cylinder. Fit the webs of both shoes into the slots of the wheel cylinder unit and then insert the end of *one* shoe into the groove of the adjuster. With the aid of the screwdriver the remaining shoe web can be eased into the slot of the adjuster unit.

Refit the drums and wheels and adjust the brakes as previously described.

It is advisable, when fitting replacement shoes, to fit a new set of pull-off springs as well.

Brake Hoses and Pipes. In some cases the cause of faulty brakes may be traced to a choked flexible hose. In view of the vital importance of the brakes, a new hose—or a set of new hoses—should be fitted if there is the slightest doubt about the condition of those in service.

It is equally important to check the condition of the brake pipelines, which are clipped to the underside of the car, at least twice a year, and especially after the car has been running on salt-laden roads during the winter. Once corrosion starts, it progresses very quickly and local pitting can become deep enough to pierce the pipe and allow brake fluid to escape. Far too little attention is paid to this very real risk during routine servicing in the average garage.

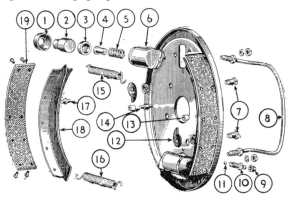

FIG. 45. TYPICAL FRONT BRAKE ASSEMBLY

1. Dust cover
2. Piston
3. Piston seal
4. Air excluder
5. Piston return spring
6. Cylinder
7. Adjuster studs
8. Connecting pipe
9. Bleed screw cap
10. Bleed screw

11. Bleed screw ball
12. Adjuster cam
13. Steady post bush
14. Steady post
15. Upper return spring
16. Lower return spring
17. Adjuster cam post
18. Brake shoe
19. Brake shoe lining

Dismantling the Brake System. Owners are advised to entrust this work to an authorized agent. However, if it is essential that the owner should carry out this work himself, the parts should be handled and assembled only under conditions of scrupulous cleanliness. A study of Figs. 45–7 will show the order in which the parts should be dismantled and reassembled.

Wheel Cylinders. The front brakes are of the two-leading-shoe type. Each cylinder is fitted with one piston and the rear end of the cylinder casting is formed to create an inclined abutment on which the shoes slide. It will be seen from Fig. 45 that each brake shoe is located on one cylinder and expanded by the piston of the other with the leading edges of both shoes making initial contact with the drums.

The exploded view clearly shows all details of the brake assembly and also the component parts of the wheel cylinders. The construction of these is simple; they consist of a housing with a highly-finished internal bore in which is assembled a light spring, a seal and seal support, a piston and a dust cover. These internal parts can be easily withdrawn when the

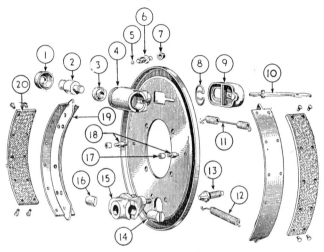

FIG. 46. REAR BRAKE ASSEMBLY

This is typical of all models, except that on later types the hydraulic cylinder is at the base of the backplate

1. Dust cover	8. Circlip	14. Tappet
2. Piston	9. Dust cover	15. Adjuster housing
3. Piston seal	10. Handbrake-actuated	16. Tappet
4. Cylinder	lever	17. Steady post bushes
5. Bleed screw ball	11. Upper return spring	18. Steady posts
6. Bleed screw	12. Lower return spring	19. Brake shoe
7. Bleed screw cap	13. Conical adjuster	20. Brake shoe lining

dust cover is removed. The bridge pipe, which passes from one cylinder to the opposite member, is situated on the reverse side of the backplate. It will be noticed that the shoe springs pass from a hole or peg situated towards the abutment end of the shoes to a hole provided in the backplate and are not fitted from shoe to shoe.

Rear Brakes. The rear brakes differ from the front in that they have one trailing-shoe and one leading-shoe in each drum. They also incorporate the sliding shoe principle, but the shoe springs are fitted from shoe to shoe. The shoes are operated hydraulically by a single cylinder of simple construction consisting of two pistons, on which the shoes locate, separated by a light compression spring and two pressure seals. To provide independent mechanical operation by the hand brake, a simple mechanical expander is assembled on the cylinder body.

Adjustment for lining wear is by means of a wedge-type mechanical adjuster. This housing is bolted securely to the backplate and contains

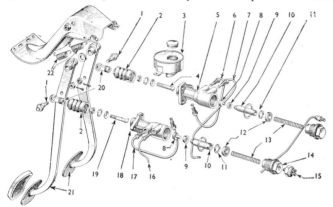

FIG. 47. CLUTCH AND BRAKE MASTER CYLINDERS (LATER TYPE)

1. Pivot	12. Seal
2. Dust excluder	13. Return spring
3. Fluid reservoir	14. End cap
4. Push rod	15. Brake-light switch
5. Clutch master cylinder	16. Pipeline to brake cylinders
6. Inlet pipeline	17. Inlet pipe
7. Pipeline to clutch servo	18. Brake master cylinder
8. Piston	19. Push rod
9. Piston seal	20. Yoke
10. Plunger	21. Pedal
11. Washer	22. Return spring

two steel links, the inclined inner faces of which locate on a hardened steel cone or wedge carried on a threaded spindle.

Provision is made on all wheel cylinders for bleeding the system. The bleed nipple screw bears upon a steel ball which is normally seated firmly on a valve opening in the cylinder. Only when the bleed screw is partially released can fluid escape.

Bleeding the Brakes. As mentioned earlier, insufficient fluid in the reservoir can result in air entering the system and making the brakes feel "spongy." If this condition is suspected, it will be necessary to bleed the air from the hydraulic system and your authorized dealer should be consulted. If such service is not readily available the work can be undertaken as follows, the reservoir being filled with the correct fluid first, and maintained at least a quarter full throughout the operation (otherwise air may be drawn in, necessitating a fresh start). There is one bleed valve on the bottom wheel cylinder of each front brake and on the expander housing (opposite the adjuster) on each rear brake. The clutch operating

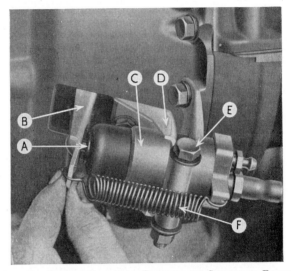

FIG. 48. CLUTCH OPERATING CYLINDER ON SIDE-VALVE ENGINES (SHOWING CLAMP BOLT THAT ALLOWS CYLINDER TO BE MOVED TO ADJUST CLEARANCE AT PUSH ROD)

A. Push-rod
B. Release arm
C. Operating cylinder
D. Mounting bracket
E. Clamp bolt
F. Retracting spring

system is separate, but the bleed valve is at the rear of the clutch operating cylinder.

Attach a rubber tube to the bleeder screw on one of the wheel cylinders and allow the free end to be submerged in a little fluid in a clean glass jar. Open the bleeder screw one complete turn. The brake pedal should be depressed slowly and allowed to return unassisted. This pumping action should be repeated with a slight pause between each operation, topping-up the reservoir as necessary. A watch should be kept on the flow of liquid in the jar and, when bubbles cease to appear, the pedal should be held down firmly and the bleeder screw securely tightened. Repeat this operation on all wheel cylinders.

After 18 months or 24,000 miles in service, the system should be drained, flushed and refilled. To do this, pump all fluid out of the system through the bleeder screw of each wheel cylinder in turn as described above.

FIG. 49. CLUTCH ADJUSTMENT ON OVERHEAD-VALVE ENGINES

A. Bleed valve
B. Operating cylinder
C. Push-rod
D. Lock-nut
E. Domed adjusting nut
F. Clutch release arm
G. Retracting spring

Refill with clean brake fluid and "bleed" the system.

After 3 years service the various units, including the pipelines, should be dismantled and thoroughly cleaned and all rubber parts, including flexible hoses, should be replaced.

THE HYDRAULIC CLUTCH

On early cars the reservoir tank for the hydraulic brake system also acts as the supply tank for the master cylinder of the hydraulic clutch release mechanism. Separate reservoirs are provided on later models (Fig. 6). Provided that the reservoir is kept topped up to the correct level, no other attention should be required. Should air enter the system, however, the clutch will be difficult to disengage. This will entail bleeding the system, an operation which should be carried out in a similar manner to that of bleeding a wheel cylinder in the braking system. The bleeder screw is at the rear of the clutch operating cylinder.

If the clutch squeals during the first few pedal depressions after a cold start, the noise is not a symptom of impending trouble. It is caused by a dry spigot bearing in the end of the crankshaft, and can be ignored until it is necessary to remove the gearbox for some other attention.

Clutch Adjustment. The only other attention required by the clutch release mechanism is to check the amount of free travel at the clutch release arm. On side-valve engined models it should be $\frac{1}{10}$ in. (2·5 mm) (early cars) or $\frac{1}{16}$ in. (1·6 mm) (later models). It should be obtained by adjusting the position of the operating cylinder as shown in Fig. 48.

After releasing the cylinder clamping bolt, the operating cylinder may be shifted backwards or forwards to adjust the clearance between the push rod and the clutch release arm.

On the overhead-valve engined models, the clearance should be $\frac{1}{16}$ in. It is adjusted by disconnecting the release arm return spring, slackening the lock-nut on the operating rod and turning the domed adjusting nut at the end of the push-rod clockwise in order to increase the free movement and anti-clockwise to reduce it. The mechanism is shown in Fig. 49.

As the adjusting nut tends to rust and bind on its threads, difficulty in carrying out the adjustment can be forestalled by lubricating the push-rod and nut during the 5,000-mile (8,000-km) service.

7 Suspension, steering and tyres

THE front suspension on all models is of the independent type and consists of coil spring suspension units incorporating built-in hydraulic double-acting shock absorbers.

To top-up the front suspension units on later models the car should first be parked, unladen, on level ground. The combined filler and level plug is located in the tube, just below the coil spring seating, at the front or rear of the unit. The correct shock absorber fluid should be added until the level reaches the bottom of the plug hole. On, earlier models no provision is made for topping-up, the complete unit being sealed at the works.

If there is a knocking noise from the front of the car when driving over rough road surfaces, the bearing races at the upper ends of the front suspension struts may be worn. If they are found to be dry they should be lubricated (see page 16) but if this does not cure the noise or the races are rusty, new bearings must be fitted. This is a job for a Ford dealer as it is difficult to remove the large retaining nuts without the correct tool.

Another fault to look for is perishing of the rubber bush surrounding the top of the strut. If the strut is protruding through this bush, a new assembly will be required. A third weak point on older cars is rusting of the metal around the point at which the strut is bolted to the wing. If rust is allowed to go unchecked, the strut will eventually burst through the wing, possibly with serious consequences if the car should be travelling at any appreciable speed. Some Ford dealers forestall this risk by reinforcing the attachment point with a welded plate.

The rear semi-elliptic springs should be regularly cleaned and sprayed or brushed with penetrating oil. The synthetic rubber inserts between the leaves are oil and grease resistant.

A periodic inspection of the rear spring U-bolts should be made to ensure that all accessible bolts and nuts are fully tightened.

When telescopic, cylindrical shock absorbers are fitted at the rear, these require no attention. Lever-type shock absorbers can be topped-up (*see* page 16), but if the level falls appreciably between services, the shock absorbers must be leaking, indicating general deterioration and loss of efficiency which calls for renewal of the units. Modern shock absorbers seldom have a life exceeding 25–35,000 miles (40–56,000 km). Worn shock absorbers affect both steering and roadholding and it is therefore dangerous to postpone renewal of these vital suspension components.

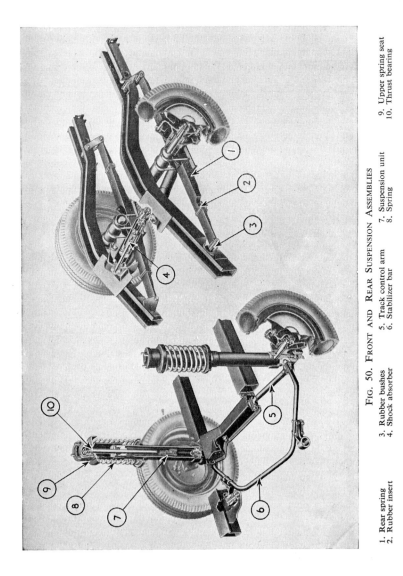

Fig. 50. Front and Rear Suspension Assemblies

1. Rear spring	5. Track control arm	9. Upper spring seat
2. Rubber insert	6. Stabilizer bar	10. Thrust bearing
3. Rubber bushes	7. Suspension unit	
4. Shock absorber	8. Spring	

FRONT WHEEL BEARINGS

Occasionally the front wheels should be jacked up and the bearings should be tested by grasping the tyre at the top and bottom and rocking the wheel vertically about the hub. Do not confuse any possible looseness which may exist in the various steering connexions with wheel bearing play; watch for relative movement between the brake drum and brake backplate.

If it has been determined that excessive play exists in the front wheel bearings these should be adjusted as described on pages 14–6.

Cleanliness is most essential when dealing with all types of bearings. The car should never be run with the grease caps missing since this would allow grit and other road dirt to enter the bearings. The front hub grease retainer should be renewed if necessary.

STEERING GEAR

On Anglia models from September 1959 onwards, the steering gearbox is of the worm and nut type, friction being kept to the minimum by the use of recirculating ball bearings between the worm and the nut. When wear develops in this unit it will be necessary to remove shims from beneath the end plate or top coverplate. To carry out the work effectively entails removal of the steering gearbox and column, so that the job is best left to a Ford dealer.

On the Prefects, Populars and earlier Anglias, however, the steering gear is of the worm and ball-peg type, consisting of a single-start worm attached to the bottom of the centre steering column and supported on two ball-races. A split bush is fitted at the top of the column to provide a further support for the steering shaft. This does not usually require further attention. End-float which may develop in the steering shaft is taken up by varying the number or thickness of the shims seen under the end plate in Fig. 51. The adjuster seen in Fig. 3 takes up end-float in the rocker shaft.

Satisfactory steering depends not only on the condition of the steering gearbox and connexions, but also on the maintenance of the correct steering angles and geometry of the whole of the front suspension and steering assembly. For example, if these angles are upset as a result of a minor kerb collision, the steering will be adversely affected and tyre wear may be greatly increased. Because the steering angles are determined by the initial assembly of the parts, accurate checking of the adjustment of these angles is beyond the scope of the owner. If the steering is unsatisfactory or tyre wear is rapid, the car should be taken to an authorized Ford service agent for expert attention.

To take a concrete example, let us consider the adjustment of the toe-in of the front wheels, just referred to above. This adjustment is extremely critical, since the toe-in should never exceed $\frac{1}{8}$ in. nor be less than $\frac{1}{16}$ in. ($3 \cdot 17$–$1 \cdot 56$ mm). This dimension is the difference between the distance measured between the front wheels behind the axle at hub height, and then between the wheels in front of the axle, also at hub height.

It will be obvious that where such a precise measurement is concerned, it is essential to use an accurate trammel or preferably a modern optical gauge.

Steering Gear Adjustments. If wear develops in the steering gearbox of a pre-September 1959 model, it is a simple matter to reduce the end-float on the rocker shaft by means of the screw and lock-nut shown in Figs. 3 and 51. Before carrying out this adjustment the connexions on the steering arms and tubes should be carefully checked over to make sure that looseness in one or more of these joints is not causing the trouble.

It is essential to set the front wheels in the straight-ahead position when testing the movement of the steering wheel, since the steering gear is so designed that an increasing degree of clearance between the peg and the worm is provided as full lock is approached in either direction. This allows adjustment to be taken up over the small central range over which the great majority of steering movements take place, without causing stiffness over the less worn sections towards full lock in either direction.

Jack up the front wheels and thoroughly grease the steering connections. With the wheels set straight-ahead there should be only a slight free

STEERING FAULTS

Symptom	Probable Cause
Heavy Steering	Low pressures in front tyres.
	Inadequate lubricant in steering unit and/or joints.
	Incorrect steering adjustments.
Excessive Free Movement at Steering Wheel	Wear in steering linkage. The outer ball joints are, self-adjusting and if slackness develops they should be renewed.
	Wear in steering gearbox assembly. Adjustment by a Ford dealer may correct this. Otherwise fit a reconditioned assembly.
	Steering unit mounting bolts slack.
Steering Wander	Low or uneven tyre pressures. If the rear tyre pressures are too low, the car will "oversteer" and will be affected by side winds at speeds.
A tendency to wander and general lack of precision may be caused by slackness at any point in the steering gear (*see* above). Otherwise, check for faults in the next column.	Steering geometry incorrect. Have the geometry checked by a service station which possesses first-class modern equipment.
	Distortion or damage to steering or suspension units. This may be caused by a minor collision and will be revealed by checks, carried out with precision equipment, against the measurements specified in the workshop manual. Normally a job for the expert.
Wheel Wobble or Steering Vibration at Speed	Unbalanced wheels and tyres will cause vibration, often at about 60–70 m.p.h. Have wheels and tyres checked both for static and dynamic balance.
	Incorrect steering geometry. See "Steering Wander," above.
	Slackness in steering gear. See "Excessive Free Movement at Steering Wheel," above.
	Weak shock absorbers.

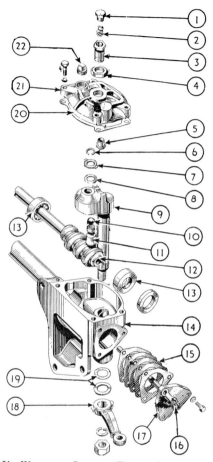

FIG. 51. WORM AND BALL-PEG TYPE OF STEERING GEARBOX

1. Adjuster screw bolt
2. Spring
3. Adjuster screw
4. Locking nut
5. Ball peg adjuster
6. Circlip
7. Locking washer
8. Plain washer
9. Rocker shaft
10. Ball
11. Rocker shaft ball peg

12. Worm
13. Steering gear shaft bearing
14. Steering gear housing
15. Adjusting shims
16. Traffic indicator tube clamp
17. End plate
18. Drop arm
19. Oil seal and washer
20. Cover gasket
21. Steering box cover
22. Oil filter plug

movement of the steering wheel. If the movement is excessive, the adjuster locking nut should be slackened and the adjuster screwed down until free movement at the steering wheel is just eliminated. This adjustment should not be overdone and when the steering wheel is turned from lock to lock with the front wheels jacked up, there should be no perceptible tight spot as the central position is reached and passed.

Provided that the steering gearbox is kept topped up with the correct grade of oil and tyre pressures are maintained at the correct figures, the steering should remain satisfactory for many thousands of miles.

The Macpherson-strut front suspension used on these cars, however, is particularly sensitive to lack of balance of the front wheels and tyres. If wheel-wobble or vibration occurs at speeds from about 40 m.p.h. (64 k.p.h.) upwards, have the balance of the front wheels checked by a competent tyre specialist. If the trouble persists after balancing the wheels, look for wear in the bottom ball-joint assemblies of the suspension struts. Other causes of poor steering are incorrect tyre pressures, uneven tyre wear, wear in the steering connections, weak shock absorbers and incorrect steering geometry.

TYRES AND TUBES

Apart from incorrect steering geometry and wheel alignment, the most usual cause of excessive tyre wear is under-inflation of the tyres. Although some increase in comfort can be obtained by running the tyres at lower pressures than those recommended, this can be done only at the expense of tyre wear and also results in deterioration in road-holding and braking.

When the pressure is too low, undue bending and flexing of the tyre walls occur. In addition the tread becomes worn on the outer edges, while the centre remains comparatively unworn. The rate of tread wear is consequently increased, owing to the fact that wear is not distributed evenly over the whole of the tread.

The necessity for checking the tyre pressures at weekly intervals when tubeless tyres are not fitted will be appreciated when it is understood that every normal inner tube, even when new, loses pressure at the rate of from 1 to 3 lb (0·07–0·21 kg) per week, owing to a process known as "diffusion." Oxygen from the air in the tyre is absorbed by rubber and a corresponding amount of oxygen is given off from the outer surface of the tube. It is necessary, therefore, to restore this slight loss of pressure even when the tubes are in first-class condition.

An advantage of tubeless tyres is that they are not subject to this diffusion, since the casings are much thicker than a conventional inner tube. Alternatively, synthetic tubes can be obtained which do not lose pressure in this manner. Nevertheless, pressures should be checked regularly as a precautionary measure.

A disadvantage of tubeless tyres from the owner's point of view is that it is difficult to obtain the initial seal between the beads of the tyre and the flanges of the rim, unless a garage airline is available. The garage method is to remove the centre from the valve and apply the airline so that the rush of air springs the beads of the tyre against the rim, providing a satisfactory air seal. The valve core is then replaced and the tyre inflated in the normal manner. It will be obvious that if an owner attempts to expand a tyre by using only a hand-pump or foot-pump there will be insufficient volume of air available to produce an effective seal.

FIG. 52. JACKING THE CAR
On later models a ratchet-action handle is used

In an emergency, however, it is possible to expand the beads of the tyre against the flanges of the wheel rim by compressing the centre of the tread inwards. At a service station, this is done by applying a metal tourniquet to the tyre. An improvised scheme is to wrap a length of rope around the tread of the tyre, forming a loop in it and then twisting the loop tightly with a short bar. With the tread compressed in this manner sufficient air should be pumped into the tyre by really vigorous—or desperate!—use of the tyre pump to raise the pressure to about 5–10 lb per sq in. (0.35–0.7 kg/cm^2), after which the tourniquet can be safely removed and the tyre inflated to well above its normal pressure—say, 50 lb per sq in. (3.5 kg/cm^2) —in order to seat the beads firmly against the flanges. If a water tank is available it is advisable to check the tyre for leakage. Alternatively, lay the tyre on the ground and brush a solution of soapy water around the joint between the rim and the bead of the tyre in order to detect any bubbles caused by leakage. The tyre should then be turned over and the process repeated on the other rim.

Do not forget, of course, to reduce the pressure in the tyre to the correct figure as quoted in Chapter 8.

If a tubeless tyre is repaired by "plugging," this should be regarded only as a temporary measure. Speed should be kept down to 50 m.p.h. (80 k.p.h.) and a proper vulcanized repair should be be made as soon as possible.

8 Facts and figures

SOME of the details given in the following pages appear elsewhere in this book, but they have been summarized here for ease of reference.

In these data tables it is necessary to distinguish between the range of cars fitted with side-valve engines—the Anglia and Prefect up to September, 1959, and the Popular from September, 1959, onwards—and the overhead-valve engined Anglia and Prefect, introduced in September and October, 1959 respectively.

The earlier Anglia and Prefect range and the Popular will be dealt with first. The tables for the later (105E and 107E) Anglias and Prefects will be found on pages 109–11, and those for the Anglia Super and the 1,000 cc. and 1,200 cc. o.h.v. vans on pages 112 and 113.

ANGLIA AND PREFECT TO SEPTEMBER 1959. POPULAR FROM SEPTEMBER 1959 ONWARDS (100E ENGINE)

GENERAL DATA

Engine.	.	Four-cylinder, side-valve.
Bore	.	2·5 in. (63·5 mm).
Stroke	.	3·64 in. (92·5 mm).
Cubic capacity	.	71·55 cu in. (1,172 c.c.).
Compression ratio		7:1.
Brake horse-power (maximum)	.	36 at 4,500 r.p.m.
Cylinder head	.	Detachable cast-iron.
Valves	.	Side-valves operated from chain-driven camshaft.
Valve clearance (cold)	.	0·0115–0·0135 in. (0·29–0·34 mm).
Lubrication system		Full pressure feed by submerged gear-type pump to main camshaft and connecting-rod bearings. By-pass type external filter. Pressure-relief valve in pump.
Cooling system	.	Pressurized. Belt-driven, two-blade fan and water pump. Thermostatic control.
Engine number	.	Stamped on left-hand side of cylinder block near oil filter tube; except later Anglia and Escort—stamped on right-hand side of cylinder block, immediately above generator mounting bracket.
Chassis number	.	Stamped around the right-hand suspension unit upper mounting and is the same as engine number.

CAPACITIES

	IMP. PT	U.S. PT	LITRES
Engine sump			
inc. filter, from April, 1955 . .	4½	5·4	2·56
inc. filter, before April, 1955 . .	5¼	6·3	3·0
exc. filter	3½	4·2	1·98
Gear box	1¾	2·1	0·95
Rear axle			
from April, 1955 . . .	1½	1·8	0·85
early models	1	1·2	0·57

	IMP. GAL	U.S. GAL	LITRES
Cooling system	1½	1·8	6·82
Fuel tank			
vans	5½	6·6	25·0
other models	7	8·4	31·8

CARBURETTOR SETTINGS—CARS

Idling jet	50
Main jet	110
Starter jet . . .	130*
Idling air bleed . . .	1·2 mm
Starter air jets . .	5 mm
Main air correction jet . .	160
Choke tube diameter . .	21 mm

CARBURETTOR SETTINGS—VANS

	Prior to Dec. 1955	After Dec. 1955	After Jan. 1956 (5 cwt. Van only)
Idling jet	50	50	50
Main jet	110	110	95
Starter jet	130	120	120
Idling air bleed . . .	1·20 mm	1·20 mm	1·20 mm
Starter air jet . . .	5 mm	5 mm	5 mm
Main air correction jet .	160	160	185
Choke tube diameter . .	21 mm	21 mm	18 mm

* Size 120 after November, 1955.

IGNITION

System   .   .   .   . Coil and distributor.
Initial timing   .   .   . Top-dead centre

Sparking plugs—

    type   .   .   .   . Champion L-10, Lodge CN (14 mm)
    gap   .   .   .   . 0·025 in. (0·64 mm)

Firing order   .   .   . 1, 2, 4, 3

Contact-breaker points gap . 0·014–0·016 in. (0·36–0·41 mm)

TRANSMISSION

Clutch release arm movement—

    late models   .   .   .   . $\frac{1}{10}$ in. (2·54 mm)
    early models   .   .   .   . $\frac{1}{16}$ in. (1·6 mm)

Overall gear ratios—All Models		1st	2nd	3rd	Rev.
prior to August, 1955	. .	15·07	8·25	4·429	19·71
August, 1955, onwards	. .	16·23	8·89	4·429	21·22

SUSPENSION, STEERING AND TYRES

Front suspension .   . Built-in independent front-wheel suspension. Directly-operated coil springs. Hydraulic double-acting shock absorbers. Stabilizer bar incorporated.
Castor angle   .   . $1°-2° 30'$
Camber angle   .   . $0° 45'-2° 15'$
King-pin inclination   . $3° 30'-5°$
Toe-in   .   .   . $\frac{1}{16}-\frac{1}{8}$ in. (1·6–3·2 mm)
Steering gear ratio   . 11·5 : 1

Tyre sizes
    cars   .   .   . 5·20 × 13 in. (5·60 × 13 in. optional equipment)
    Escort, Squire, vans . 5·60 × 13 in.
Tyre pressures   .   . 24 lb per sq in. (1·687 kg per sq cm), front and rear, all models except 7-cwt van: rear tyres 28 lb per sq in. (1·97 kg per sq cm) on this model.

BATTERY

Voltage .   .   .   .   .   . 12 V
Capacity   .   .   .   .   . 40 amp-hr at 20 hr rate
Terminal earthed   .   .   .   . Positive
Specific gravity (fully charged) .   . 1·270–1·285 at 70°F (21°C)

LAMP BULBS

Headlamp—

U.K.	50/40 W prefocus
export	36/36 W or 45/35 W prefocus

Sidelamp and front direction indicator,
rear and stop . . . . 21/6 W double contact, offset pin
Rear direction indicator . . . 21 W double contact, offset pin
Panel lamps . . . . 2·2 W miniature bayonet cap
      Popular, 2·2 W, M.E.S.
Panel warning lamps . . 2·2 W miniature bayonet cap
Number plate . . . . 6 W single contact
Interior light (when fitted) . . 6 W festoon

DIMENSIONS

	CARS	ESCORT, SQUIRE AND VAN
Length . . .	12 ft 7¼ in. (384·2 cm)	Approx. 11 ft 7 in. (353 cm)—11 ft 10¼ in. (360 cm)
Width	5 ft 0½ in. (153·5 cm)	5 ft 0¾ in. (154 cm)
Height . . .	Approx. 4 ft 11 in. (150 cm)	5 ft 3 in. (160 cm)
Ground clearance . .	7 in. (19 cm)	7 in. (19 cm)
Wheel base . .	7 ft 3 in. (221 cm)	7 ft 3 in. (221 cm)
Turning circle . .	34 ft 6 in. (10·52 m)	34 ft 6 in. (10·52 m)
Early Anglia and Prefect	33 ft 6 in. (10·2 m)	
Track—front . .	4 ft (122 cm)	4 ft (122 cm)
Track—rear . . .	3 ft 11½ in. (120·7 cm)	3 ft 11½ in. (120·7 cm)

KERB WEIGHTS (WITH STANDARD EQUIPMENT)

Approx.

Early Anglia	1,618 lb (733·9 kg)
Late Anglia . . .	1,699 lb (770·7 kg)
Anglia De Luxe . . .	1,716 lb (778·4 kg)
Early Prefect . . .	1,670 lb (757·5 kg)
Late Prefect . . .	1,751 lb (794·3 kg)
Popular	1,668 lb (756·6 kg)
Late Prefect De Luxe .	1,765 lb (800·6 kg)
Escort, Squire . . .	1,804 lb (818·0 kg)
Van, 5 cwt . . .	1,563 lb (709·6 kg)
Van, 7 cwt . . .	1,640 lb (743·9 kg)

ANGLIA 105E, SEPTEMBER 1959 ONWARDS
PREFECT 107E, OCTOBER 1959 ONWARDS

GENERAL DATA

Engine . . .	. Four-cylinder, overhead valve
Bore . . .	. 3·1875 in. (80·963 mm)
Stroke . . .	. 1·906 in. (48·412 mm)
Cubic capacity. .	. 60·84 in. (996·6 c.c.)
Compression ratio .	. 8·9:1 (standard, for premium grade fuel)
	7·5:1 (optional, for regular grade fuel)
Valves . . .	. Vertical overhead type; push-rod operated
Valve clearance .	. 0·010 in. (0·254 mm) inlet
	0·017 in. (0·432 mm) exhaust
	(Normal running temperature)
Firing order . .	. 1, 2, 4, 3
Max. brake horse power	.
(nett) . . .	. 39 at 5,000 r.p.m. (8·9 c.r.)
	37 at 5,000 r.p.m. (7·5 c.r.)
Maximum torque .	. 52·85 lb ft at 2,700 r.p.m. (8·9 c.r.)
	50·43 lb ft at 2.700 r.p.m. (7·5 c.r.)
Engine number .	. Stamped on the top face of the right-hand engine mounting pad
Chassis number .	. Stamped around the front suspension unit upper mounting on the right-hand mudguard
Cooling system .	. Pressurized thermo-siphon, impeller assisted circulation. Bellows-type thermostat in cylinder head water outlet
Radiator pressure cap	. 7 lb/sq in. (0·492 kg/sq cm)

CAPACITIES

					IMP. PT	U.S. PT	LITRES
Engine sump							
including filter	.	.	.	.	4½*	5·4*	2·56*
excluding filter	.	.	.	.	4*	4·78*	2·27*
Cooling system							
without heater	.	.	.	.	10¼	12·3	5·82
with heater	.	.	.	.	11¼	13·5	6·39
Gearbox .	.	.	.	.	1¾	2·1	0·99
Rear axle .	.	.	.	.	2	2·4	1·13
					IMP. GAL	U.S. GAL	LITRES
Fuel tank .	.	.	.	.	7	8·4	31·82

See also page 11.

CARBURETTOR

Jet sizes	Downdraught type	
	Prior to Jan. 60	After Jan. 60
Main jet	115	115
Main air correction jet . . .	175	175
Economizer jet . . .	140	140
Economizer air correction jet . .	195	195
Idling jet	50	40
Idling air correction jet . .	120	150
Starter jet	125	125
Choke tube	22 mm	22 mm

Later type of carburettor, with accelerator pump, and strangler in place of starting carburettor, May 1962 onwards—

Main jet	97·5
Main air correction jet . . .	100
Accelerator pump discharge nozzle jet . .	45
Idling air correction jet . . .	85
Idling jet	50
Choke tube	21·5 mm

RECOMMENDED FUEL

High-compression engines require "Premium" fuel, but a "Mixture" grade is often suitable. "Super" petrols are not necessary but can be used if desired. Low-compression engines can be run on "Regular" grade.

IGNITION SYSTEM

Type   .   .   .   . Coil and distributor. Automatic control by governor weight mechanism combined with vacuum control from induction manifold.

Initial advance .   .   . 10° (crankshaft), high and low compression

Sparking plugs

type   .   .   . . Autolite AG22 or Champion N-9Y (14 mm)
gap   .   .   . . 0·023 in. to 0·028 in. (0·59 to 0·71 mm)

Contact-breaker gap—*see* also page 54

Lucas distributor   . . 0·014 in. to 0·016 in. (0·356 to 0·406 mm)
Autolite distributor . 0·025 in. (0·635 mm)

STEERING, SUSPENSION AND TYRES

Turning circle . .	.	32 ft 0 in. (9·75 m)
Front suspension .	.	Independent, coil spring suspension, embodying built-in, double-acting hydraulic shock absorbers.
Rear suspension .	.	Longitudinal, semi-elliptic springs
Castor angle . .	.	1°30′ to 3° 0′
Camber angle .	.	0° 30′ to 2° 0′
Toe-in . . .	.	$\frac{1}{8}$ in. to $\frac{3}{16}$ in. (3·175 to 4·76 mm)
Toe-in on 20° turns .	.	1° 36′ to 3° 6′
King-pin inclination .	.	4° 45′ to 6° 15′
Track . . .	.	46 in. (116·6 cm)

Car unladen

Tyres—Saloons .	.	Tubeless, 5·20 × 13, 4-ply (5·60 × 13 optional on Prefect)
Pressures –front and rear .		Anglia: 22 lb/sq in. (1·54 kg/sq cm) Prefect: 24 lb/sq in. (1·687 kg/sq cm)
Tyres—Estate cars .	.	Tubeless 5·60 × 13
Pressures . .	.	Front 24 lb/sq in. (1·687 kg/sq cm) Rear 30 lb/sq in. (2·109 kg/sq cm)

LAMP BULBS (ALL 12-VOLT)

	Wattage
Head lamp	50/40
Side and front direction indicator .	21/6
Rear and stop light . . .	21/6
Rear direction indicator . .	21
Interior lamp	3
Rear number plate . . .	6
Instrument panel . . .	2·2
Direction indicator warning light .	2·2
Generator warning light . .	2·2
Oil pressure warning light . .	2·2
Headlight beam warning light . .	2·2

WEIGHTS AND DIMENSIONS

	ANGLIA	PREFECT	ANGLIA ESTATE CAR
Wheelbase . .	7 ft 6½ in. (230 cm)	7 ft 3 in. (221 cm)	7 ft 6½ in. (230 cm)
Overall length .	12 ft 9½ in. (390 cm)	12 ft 5¾ in. (380·4 cm)	12 ft 10¼ in. (392 cm)
Overall width .	4 ft 9¾ in. (145 cm)	5 ft 0¾ in. (154·3 cm)	4 ft 9⅝ in. (145 cm)
Kerb weight .	1,634 lb (761·1 kg)	1,768 lb (801·9 kg)	1,792 lb (812 kg)
Ground clearance .	6·4 in. (16·3 cm)	6·4 in. (16·3 cm)	6·4 in. (16·3 cm)

ANGLIA SUPER 123E

The Anglia Super, introduced in September, 1962, is fitted with a 1,200 c.c. engine. It has the all-synchromesh four-speed gearbox designed for the Classic and Capri and subsequently used also in the Cortina. To handle the additional performance provided by the larger engine, it has wider brake drums. It is identified by a special flash on the body side and by anodized aluminium wheel trims, and has a number of interior refinements such as better seats, a padded facia, a cigar lighter, screen washers, twin horns, and an interior heater.

MAIN DIFFERENCES IN SPECIFICATION
(Otherwise as pages 109–11)

ENGINE

Stroke . . .	. 2·29 in. (58·17 mm)
Cubic capacity . .	. 73·09 cu in. (1,198 c.c.)
Compression ratio .	. 8·7:1 standard; 7·3:1 optional
Maximum b.h.p. (nett)	. 48·5 at 4,800 r.p.m. (8·7:1)
	46 at 4,800 r.p.m. (7·3:1)
Maximum torque .	. 63 lb ft at 2,700 r.p.m. (8·7:1)
	60 lb ft at 2,700 r.p.m. (7·3:1)

FUEL SYSTEM

Jet sizes

Main jet	. 110
Main air correction jet .	. 200
Accelerator pump jet .	. 40
Idling jet . . .	. 50
Economy jet . . .	. 65
Choke tube diameter .	. 33 mm
Needle valve . . .	. 1·6 mm

IGNITION SYSTEM

Initial advance . 6° b.t.d.c. (crankshaft), high and low compression

5-CWT AND 7-CWT VANS FITTED WITH
1,000 c.c. AND 1,200 c.c. OVERHEAD-VALVE ENGINES

The basic specifications of these models are similar to those of the Anglia, Anglia Super and Prefect given on pages 109 to 112. Only the essential differences, therefore, are given below.

ENGINE DATA
 Compression Ratio
    1,000 c.c. model, September 1963 onwards   . 8·0:1 (standard)
                  Prior to September 1963   . 7·5:1 (standard)
                                     8·9:1 (optional)
    1,200 c.c. model .   .   .   .   .   . 8·7:1 (standard)

FUEL SYSTEM
Recommended fuel .   . Regular, for standard cylinder head. Premium for higher-compression cylinder head.
Fuel tank capacity .   . 6 Imp gal (7·2 U.S. gal, 27·12 litres)

IGNITION SYSTEM—1,000 C.C. MODEL
        Initial advance   .   .   . $8°$ (crankshaft)
        Prior to September 1963 .   . $10°$ (crankshaft)

STEERING GEOMETRY
        Castor   .   .   . $3°$ $3'$
        Camber   .   .   . $1°$
        King-pin inclination . $5°$ $36'$
        Toe-in   .   .   . $\frac{1}{8}-\frac{3}{16}$ in. (3·175–4·8 mm)

WHEELS AND TYRES
Tyres 5-cwt .   . 5·60 × 13, 4-ply tubeless (standard)
     7-cwt .   . 5·60 × 13, 6-ply tubeless (standard)
                  (5- and 7-cwt options are tubed tyres and white sidewalls)
Pressures 5-cwt   . Front and rear, 24 lb/sq in. (1·68 kg/sq cm)
        7-cwt   . Front, 24 lb/sq in. (1·68 kg/sq cm)
                Rear, 30 lb/sq in. (2·1 kg/sq cm)

WEIGHTS AND DIMENSIONS
Overall length .   .   .   . 12 ft 6$\frac{1}{4}$ in. (381 cm), without rear bumpers
                            12 ft 7$\frac{3}{4}$ in. (385 cm), with rear bumpers
Overall width .   .   .   . 4 ft 11 in. (150 cm)
Overall height, unladen   . 5 ft 4 in. (162·4 cm)
              laden   . 5 ft 1$\frac{1}{2}$ in. (156·2 cm)
Ground clearance   .   . 6·7 in. approx. (17 cm)
Kerb weight, 1,000 c.c.—5-cwt. . 1,636 lb (742 kg)
                  7-cwt . 1,674 lb (759 kg)
        1,200 c.c.—5-cwt . 1,667 lb (756·2 kg)
                  7-cwt . 1,705 lb (773 kg)

RECOMMENDED LUBRICANTS

(All Models, Anglia, Anglia Super, New Prefect, New Popular and Vans)

ENGINE

Any good quality branded oil may be used: e.g. Castrol, Esso, Shell, B.P., Mobil, Regent, Vigzol, Duckham's.

Grades—

Temperatures above 32°F (summer and winter)	. S.A.E. 20W. Alternatively a multigrade oil, S.A.E. 10W/30, 10W/40 or 20W/50
32°F to − 10°F	. S.A.E. 10W grade
Below − 10°F .	. S.A.E. 10W grade with addition of 10% Kerosene; or S.A.E. 5W

AIR CLEANER, ENGINE BREATHER, DISTRIBUTOR, DYNAMO

Appropriate engine oil.

GEARBOX

Extreme-pressure (hypoid) gear oil, S.A.E. grade 80EP.

STEERING GEARBOX

Extreme-pressure gear oil, S.A.E. 90EP.

REAR AXLE

Extreme-pressure hypoid gear oil, S.A.E. 90EP in summer and in winter temperatures above −10°F. Below −10°F use S.A.E. 80EP.

UNIVERSAL JOINTS

S.A.E. 250EP or lithium-base multi-purpose grease.

FRONT-WHEEL HUBS, REAR-WHEEL BEARINGS, STEERING GREASE NIPPLES, HANDBRAKE CABLES

Multi-purpose lithium-base grease, *preferably treated with colloidal graphite or molybdenum disulphide.*

REAR SPRINGS

Penetrating oil or used engine oil.

DOOR LOCKS, HINGES, THROTTLE LINKAGE, ETC.

Thin oil or light engine oil.

CLUTCH AND BRAKE FLUID RESERVOIRS

Castrol Girling Brake and Clutch Fluid (amber).

FRONT SUSPENSION UNIT AND SHOCK ABSORBERS WHEN FITTED WITH FILLER PLUGS

Approved shock absorber fluid obtainable from Ford dealers.

Index